JOY
in the
JOURNEY

GWENDORA MAGEE

"Joy in the Journey," by Gwendora Magee. ISBN 978-1-951985-50-9 (softcover).

Published 2020 by Virtualbookworm.com Publishing Inc., P.O. Box 9949, College Station, TX 77842, US. ©2020, Gwendora Magee. All rights reserved. No part of this publication may be reproduced, stored in a retrieval system, or transmitted in any form or by any means, electronic, mechanical, recording or otherwise, without the prior written permission of Gwendora Magee.

FOREWORD

This book is about the journey that my husband and I traveled during our 62 years of marriage. On this journey with us were our daughter Juanita, son-in-law Steven Johnson, and their three children: Jennifer Jean Johnson, William Derry "Bill" Johnson, and Ross Melvin Johnson. As Bill's wife Kellye and their four children (Mia, Chase, Berkley, and Cruze) joined the family, the journey became more exciting. Stories in this book explain how values were shared with our family and friends.

THANKS

Special thanks to our daughter Juanita (Nita) and husband Steven Johnson and their family for sharing some personal stories. Special thanks to Derry's niece, Dr. Robin Fabre Ellison and Nita who wrote a daily report to family and friends on Derry's medical condition following his stroke on Friday, December 30, 2011. A special appreciation for the technological support that Robin's children, Joshua and Lauren Ellison, provided.

DEDICATION

This book is dedicated to the memory of my deceased husband, Dr. Derry David Magee, our daughter Juanita Elaine Magee Johnson, her husband Steven Johnson, and their three children: Jennifer Jean Johnson, William Derry "Bill" Johnson (wife Kellye and children Mia, Chase, Berkley, and Cruze) and Ross Melvin Johnson.

JOY IN THE JOURNEY

Beginning the Journey

"LIFE IS A JOURNEY, NOT A DESTINATION." During a journey, one will travel over hills and valleys, smooth and bumpy roads, experience happiness and sadness. Joy comes in good times and bad times. The Bible gives us the Word from God, *"A Man sets his plan, and the Lord directs his steps." Proverbs 16:9.* The power in His Word changes us and helps us to take the path that will glorify Him as we travel on this journey to reach our destination.

Derry David Magee was born on July 5, 1934, in New Orleans, La. to Marvin Mangum Magee and Mary Bridges Magee. He had two siblings: a brother Marvin Mangum Magee, Jr. (infant death), and a sister Mary Jane Magee.

Gwendora Wilkes Magee was born on September 1, 1936 in Washington Parish, La. the second daughter of Earl Samuel Wilkes and Willie Marie Burch Wilkes. Siblings include Bobbie Earl, Dorothy Elaine, Faye Ellen, Janice Marie, Kathy (deceased), and Earl Samuel Wilkes.

As a 12 year old boy, Derry knew that he wanted to become a veterinarian. His father Rev. Marvin Magee had accepted a call to pastor his first church at Line Creek Baptist Church in Kentwood, La. The family left their home in New Orleans, La. to begin their ministry in the Line Creek Community. The Line Creek Church members loved Bro. Magee's family, and the Magee family loved the people in the Line Creek Community.

Derry's daddy informed him that he would not be able to send him to college to become a veterinarian. This country church provided Bro. Magee a small salary and the members generously shared meats and garden vegetables to supplement their income.

Derry began at age 12 finding ways to make money to finance his education. Some of the dairy farmers in the church traded Derry's dairy calves for Collie puppies. After three years, Derry had raised several heifers that would soon become a dairy herd.

During Derry's sophomore year, his father accepted a call to become the pastor at the Mt. Hermon Baptist Church. Derry's calves had grown, become heifers, and later milk cows requiring the need for a barn for milking the cows and land for growing feed.

Derry rented and later purchased a dairy farm two miles from where he and his family lived in Mt. Hermon. He rode his horse from his home each morning to milk the cows, rode back home, bathed, ate breakfast, and attended classes across the highway at Mt. Hermon High School. After school, he repeated this routine riding his horse to the farm, milking the cows, and completing the chores of feeding the cows and maintaining the milk barn.

Obtaining a formal education has always been a high priority for our family. The pursuit of a higher degree of learning was very important for us, our daughter, and her family. We enjoyed the time and resources that we spent in seeing that our family reached their educational goals.

The school cafeteria…a great place to meet a life partner

DERRY AND GWENDORA BEGAN THIS JOURNEY together approximately 65 years ago where they first met as students at the Mt. Hermon High School. Gwendora did not attend school on this particular day in order to help her father cultivate the field of corn planted in Mr. Fleet Miller's pasture behind the school. At noon, Gwendora and her dad walked over to the school cafeteria to eat lunch. (There were no cafes and fast food establishments in Mt. Hermon at that time.)

Derry wrote, "Sometime after starting Mt. Hermon High School, I walked into the cafeteria and there sitting at one of the tables was the most beautiful young lady dressed in blue denim jeans, wearing a blue denim long sleeve shirt and a red bandana handkerchief tied around her neck. My! Oh! My! Who was this beautiful young lady? As fate happens, or in the fullness of God's timing, she was Gwendora Wilkes, second daughter of Mr. Earl Wilkes and Mrs. Willie Wilkes who would later become my wife. On that fateful day, she had come into the cafeteria to eat lunch while plowing her dad's corn crop planted in Mr. Fleet Miller's field behind the school yard." This was the beginning of our journey that lasted over 62 years.

Derry and Gwendora celebrated 62 years of marriage.

Gwendora and Derry Began Their Lives
as a Couple

THE GEOMETRY CLASS at MHHS is where the courtship began for Derry and Gwendora. I sat in front of Derry in the Geometry class. I felt something gently poking my back as if to get my attention. I knew that it was Derry. After class he asked me to go to the Mt. Hermon Revival with him, and I accepted. This began a two year courtship before our marriage in 1952. Soon after Derry and I began dating, he shortened my name to "Dora" because his paternal grandmother's name was Zora. I was called Dora by him and others during our 62 years of marriage.

Derry became ill during his senior year in high school and was unable to "lay by his corn." Derry's dairy farm was on my Daddy's milk route. Daddy picked up the cans of milk, delivered the milk to the processing plant in Mt. Hermon, and returned the empty cans to Derry's farm.

Evidently, daddy was aware and could see that Derry's corn needed to be laid by; otherwise, the corn would have been too tall for a tractor to complete the cultivation process. I drove our Farmall tractor with cultivation equipment to Derry's farm and "lay by his corn crop." This was the beginning of becoming a team even before we were married.

Derry graduated MHHS in 1952 as valedictorian of his senior class and began LSU during the summer to begin the two year Pre-veterinary medicine program. In the fall of 1952, we were married making our home in Baton Rouge near the LSU campus. Our only child, Juanita Elaine Magee, was born on May 3, 1953. In the fall of 1954, our family moved to College Station, TX where Derry entered the Texas A&M College of Veterinary Medicine, receiving the Doctor of Veterinary Medicine degree in May, 1958. (He did not have any college debt at the end of his six years of veterinary medicine education.)

Following his graduation from Texas A&M, we moved back to Louisiana where he began a veterinary practice in Tangipahoa Parish, practicing 32 years in the Kentwood and surrounding areas. After these years in a successful dairy cattle practice, he

4

accepted a call to join the Large Animal and Surgery Department at Texas A&M University in 1990 as a Clinical Assistant Professor. Our life stories are recorded in our first book, *A Veterinarian's Life and A Veterinarian's Wife.*

Derry and I had always had an unconditional love for each other working as a team following Christ's teachings in the New Testament. God's Word provides instruction on how I should live as a wife. We find in Ephesians 5:22-33—*"Wives, be subject to your own husbands, as to the Lord. For the husband is the head of the wife, as Christ also, is the head of the church. He Himself being the Savior of the body. But as the church is subject to Christ, so also the wives ought to be to their husbands in everything."*

When I submitted to Derry's leadership and authority, I was actually submitting to God's authority. I often remarked, "I cannot change Derry but God can." If we had an issue, I would turn him over to God. God was always faithful in helping us resolve a situation.

The following verse gave me great comfort knowing that God had given husbands some instructions, also. In verse 28, *"Husbands, love your wives, just as Christ also loved the church and gave Himself up for her...."* What woman could not submit to a husband described in these scriptures as one who loves his wife and literally lays down his life for her?

In Genesis 2:18, we read, *"And the LORD God said, it is not good that the man should be alone; I will make him an help meet for him."* Throughout our 62 years of married life, I tried to be a *help meet* to Derry. I helped him in the dairies, in his veterinary practice, supported him in his leadership roles at church, and as a faculty wife at TAMU. He supported me in all that I was responsible for as a wife, a mother, an educator, and in church and community activities.

We always enjoyed the peace and joy that came to us when we honored each other in making decisions. When we did that, we were in submission to God and received God's blessings as a couple.

Derry and I had always wanted to hang a chandelier in the dining room at Juanwood in Kentwood, La. While we were living in College Station, Texas, we shopped for two or three years looking for the right fixture. When we finally decided on one, we brought it to Louisiana and had it hung in the ceiling of the dining room. When my siblings came to our house for a family gathering, we proudly showed them the lighting fixture that we had chosen. My sister Janice Branch remarked, "You can believe they agreed on it."

Word to the wise...

WHEN DERRY AND I HAD A DESIRE for something but did not give it the careful thought, prayer and consideration for purchasing it, we suffered the consequences.

After we retired in 2007 from our teaching positions at TAMU and in the College Station ISD, we knew we wanted to do some traveling since our families lived in other states. We thought of ways we would like to travel. We looked at camper trailers which did not appeal to Derry. We visited a motor home sales office to look at motor homes and *impulsively* purchased a motor home. Derry imagined himself driving down the road while I was in the kitchen area preparing his lunch. As I was checking out the motor home, I envisioned our going to a nice quiet fishing lake to park for a few days to fish and relax. We would not have to stop at a fast food restaurant or look for a restroom on the road.

The only problem with these expectations was that there was a console between the two bucket seats in the front. It required us to locate a place to park, get out, and enter the motor home from the outside to use the kitchen or bathroom.

To get some experience driving and riding in the motor home, we traveled to a friend's land near College Station and parked for two nights. We did not have a sewer hookup or any electricity hookup. The ride in the motor home was so bumpy that I bounced around in the back. The salesman had suggested that we remove the air in the shocks. Derry did not want to do this. I did not know anything about air in the shocks, and I do not know anything about that even today.

Patrick and Jennifer Schilling and the children rode out and visited us in the motor home. The children enjoyed playing with the litter of puppies that the owners had in the yard hoping they could find good homes for them. The boys began to put pressure on their parents to take one of the puppies, but Patrick stood firm and did not give in. They already had many animals at their home in Caldwell, TX.

Sometime later, Patrick and Jennifer drove the motor home to his brother's house on Wilkes Road in Louisiana and enjoyed spending a few days there with the family. They evidently knew how to turn on the hot water heater to have hot water for bathing.

Derry and I drove the motor home to Miami, FL for Christmas one year to spend time with our daughter Nita's family. On our way down, we stopped for a night at a campground in Florida just off the interstate. We arrived during the daylight hours. We had never used the shower nor learned how to turn on the hot water heater. This was not, the place nor time, to try. We did not have TV because we had not hooked up the antenna. We were sitting or lying in the motor home hours waiting for darkness to come so that we could finally go to sleep.

We left the campground early and headed to Miami, Florida. We arrived at Nita and Steve's home in Miami during the daylight hours. We parked the RV next to their house ready to enjoy Christmas with Nita and Steve, Jennifer, Bill and Kellye, and Ross.

The Schilling family. In the back row (left to right) are David, Patrick, Jennifer and Connor. Kathryn is in front.

After a week in Miami, we headed home to College Station, TX, driving straight through Florida without stopping to rest. Just as we reached the Florida state line headed west to Louisiana,

Derry became too sick to drive. I drove us in the heavy rain through Alabama, Mississippi, and to Ponchatoula, LA and did not stop until we reached Derry's sister and brother-in-law's house in Ponchatoula where we spent the night in the motor home.

We got up the next morning to a great breakfast prepared by Jane and Noland Fabre. We left for Texas with Derry driving. As he was backing out of the Fabre's driveway, he asked me if there were anything back there. When one is buckled in a bucket seat, there is no movement to look back or around to see what is near. Noland was there making sure Derry backed out correctly and headed down the street to begin our journey back to Texas.

I knew immediately that we had made a mistake by purchasing this motor home. When we arrived home in College Station, we unloaded the motor home and drove it to the RV storage lot in Hearne, TX.

At some point, I informed Derry that I would not get back in the motor home and travel anywhere again. Very soon, we decided to take it to PPL Motor Homes in Houston and put it on their lot to sell.

Our good friend Gerald Wynn agreed to drive the motor home to Houston with Derry. I followed in our SUV. While the man at PPL was filling out the paperwork, Derry told me that he was so sick that we had to leave. I told him that we could not leave in the midst of preparing the paperwork for the sale. Gerald had taken a day off to drive the motor home to Houston, and we could not leave until the job was complete. Derry managed to suffer through the ordeal until we were ready to head back to College Station. We dropped Gerald off at his house and headed straight to CS Medical Center Emergency Room for Derry to be examined. His primary doctor who was on duty was not happy to see him in the emergency room

The motor home sold very quickly because it was almost brand new with very few miles. We only lost approximately $10,000.00 on this foolish purchase. God's grace was with us through these motor home travels. We had learned a great lesson.

I have been told that most people who enjoy owning a motor home get a great deal of pleasure in just preparing the motor

9

home for a trip. Derry was a veterinarian who had his truck serviced by a mechanic. When he was called to a farm to treat an animal, he jumped in his truck with the veterinary equipment in place in the truck. Spending time to get a motor home ready for a trip did not interest him. Our advice: *always pray and make sure God is in your plan.*

Godly Love for Family

OUR FAMILY HAS ALWAYS BEEN at the center of our thoughts, prayers, and plans for the future. Each morning, Derry prayed for God's Hedge of Protection for us, our daughter and son-in-law, our grandchildren, and great-grandchildren and asked God's protection for our siblings and their families.

Derry shared with the men in our family a prayer of protection for their families. In Romans 8:31 *"What then shall we say to these things? If God is for us, who can be against us? In vs. 34: Who is to condemn? Christ Jesus is the one who died— and more than that, was raised—who is at the right hand of God, who indeed is interceding for us."*

My mother Willie Burch Wilkes shared with me many years ago about her Uncle Ed Foil telling her that he prayed daily for her and her children. I feel so blessed to have been one of the Wilkes children who was prayed for by this uncle.

Getting to Know Our Grandchildren

AFTER NITA AND STEVE BLESSED US with grandchildren, we spent as much time with them as possible. Our names became "DeeDee" and "Do" (pronounced "Doe) to the grandchildren and to many of our close friends. To hear one of our grandchildren, granddaughter-in-law, and great-grandchildren and nephew Patrick's family address us as "DeeDee" and "Do" is the greatest sound our ears could hear.

Jennifer was born on March 16, 1978, Bill was born on February 10, 1980 and Ross was born on October 29, 1991. I had completed my teaching degree and was teaching at Kentwood High School. While Nita and Steve were living in Jackson, Miss,

I met Nita in Brookhaven, Miss. on Friday afternoon after school to get Jennifer and Bill to bring them to Kentwood for the weekend. Sunday afternoon after church, I returned them to Nita and Steve in Brookhaven which was the halfway point between Jackson and Kentwood.

While Jennifer and Bill were with us on these weekends and during summer months, we made it a priority to take them to church and to visit with their great-grandparents, uncles, aunts, and cousins so that they would get to know their family members. After Nita and Steve moved to Miami, Florida, Derry and I drove the 16 hours straight only stopping for gas and to eat.

The Magee grandchildren (left to right): Bill, Jennifer and Ross.

Derry was in a private veterinary practice and did not receive income if he was not working. We did not have the luxury of spending a week in Miami with the family. Our purpose was to visit Nita and Steve and to bring Jennifer and Bill back to Kentwood to spend two-three weeks during the summer with us. After their visit with us, I drove them to Meridian, Mississippi to meet their other grandmother Betty (Dana) Johnson who took them to Johnson City, Tennessee the following day to spend the remainder of their summer with her and Paw Paw Bill Johnson.

During the summers that Jennifer and Bill were with us at Juanwood, we invited cousins Shasta Wilkes, Trent and Traci Forrest, and Thomas Bankston and others to our home. Some cousins spent days and nights with us. Shasta's brother Brody Wilkes missed out on doing things with these cousins because he was five years younger than Shasta. Years later when Derry and I returned to Juanwood for visits, we attended Brody's motorcycle races, saw him at FBC with his parents, Chuck and Rebecca Wilkes, and saw him at their farm when we went to eat and visit with his parents.

While Derry was at work, I took Jennifer and Bill to swim at the Kentwood Aquatic Pool. They raced on their bicycles in the yard. We attended the scheduled activities at the Kentwood library. One day, I drove the cousins to Baton Rouge to pick up Traci who joined us for the drive down the river road to tour Oak Alley and other southern plantations along the Mississippi River. I had thought that we would stop for a hamburger that day, but there were no food establishments anywhere along the way. We did not find hamburgers until we reached Hammond, LA on our way home.

One day, I loaded the bicycles in the Chevy van and drove to Percy Quin State Park where the cousins spent hours riding their bicycles through the park. One summer Bill and Jennifer attended Bible School at First Baptist Church where Jennifer accepted Christ. She waited to be baptized at Wayside Baptist Church— her church in Miami. Jennifer enjoyed helping Anna Lee Alford and Diane Williams prepare for the Bible School graduation program and other activities while Bill enjoyed playing with Marshall Williams, Diane's son. Marshall and other boys a little older than Bill were fascinated by Bill's courage and ability to swim and dive. Bill dove off the high diving board at the age of five. The boys really enjoyed swimming and diving with Bill.

One day, Marshall brought his four-wheeler to Juanwood for them to ride around Juanwood's 20 acres. They had planned to camp in a tent in front of our house, but the tent was too hot. One day when Bill and Justin Fowler were walking around the edge of the woods at the edge of our yard, a snake crossed over Bill's boots. I suppose it was good that they were wearing rubber boots.

I enjoyed cooking for Derry daily, but when we had guests and family in our home, cooking became a high priority, requiring more time in the kitchen than usual. Derry was diagnosed with diverticulosis during this time and required some special food preparations. The day Diane Williams came to pick up Marshall and his four-wheeler, I was making homemade wheat bread with high fiber for Derry which impressed her.

While Jennifer and Bill were at the clinic with Derry or riding with him on calls, I used that time to cook, bake, do laundry and clean house. One of my greatest joys while working in the kitchen was observing Jennifer and Bill playing under the large dining room table with red beans feeding their imaginary horses and cows. They spent hours playing under the big table.

I took Jennifer and Bill several times to Mt. Hermon in Washington Parish to visit their great-grandparents Earl and Willie Wilkes who always grew a huge garden and watermelons. We picnicked and swam in the Silver Creek that ran through my grandfather Burch's property. There were always cousins around to play with at the Wilkes farm. We made trips to Ponchatoula for them to visit their great-grandmother "Granny Magee" and Aunt Jane and Uncle Noland, Melody, Robin, and Jody. Each month we joined a large group of Line Creek residents who picked up trash along the roadsides of the five miles from Kentwood to Line Creek. One Saturday, we had 100 Line Creek residents picking up trash while Derry bush hogged the sides of the roads from our house to Highway 51.

Jennifer and Bill spent many hours at the Kentwood Veterinary Clinic. Derry was always so patient with them and enjoyed having them at the clinic and riding with him on ambulatory calls. While Jennifer was observing through an observation glass in the office, Bill was actually on the floor in the back of the clinic helping the veterinarians bring the animals through the chute for vaccinations, dehorning and various treatments. He helped restrain the animals with a rope while the veterinarians treated the animals. He helped put the cow on the operating table for surgery. They enjoyed the farm calls with their grandfather Derry whom they called Dee Dee.

When Bill was approximately three years old visiting us for the summer at Juanwood in Kentwood, LA, he was playing in the sand in the backyard. I happened to mention "Miami" in a conversation. He loudly stated, "Do, it is not your Ami!" "It is My-Ami."

Even as a young child Bill rode with his grandfather Dee Dee to the farms to treat animals. He oberved the veterinarians in the clinic palpating cows to check for pregnancy. One day, we observed Bill in the dining room of our home reaching his hand and arm in the central vacumn cleaner receptacle stating, "I'm 'shecking' the cows."

Jennifer enjoyed spending time in the front office with Lesia Dean who ran the office. One summer, I was puzzled why Jennifer brought with her a suitcase full of small stuffed animals from Miami to Juanwood. I soon learned! These animals were the animals that she and Shasta were going to treat at their "Kentwood Veterinary Clinic" set up in one of the upstairs bedrooms. They placed signs made of tissues at the back entrance of the house and at the top of the stairs with arrows pointing the direction for clients to bring their animals to their office. They used the telephone upstairs to call clients to make appointments and to remind clients to pay their bills. Evidently, Jennifer had picked up some tips on operating a veterinary practice while spending time with Lesia in the office.

The Johnson family. In the back row (left to right) are Jennifer, Steve, Bill and Ross. In the front are Nita, Mia and Kellye (who is holding Chase).

The Journey Continues

OUR JOURNEY CONTINUED as we left Kentwood in 1990 to begin new careers in College Station, TX. Derry accepted a teaching position in the Large Animal & Surgery Department of the Texas A&M College of Veterinary Medicine in College Station, TX. I accepted a teaching position in the College Station ISD.

The grandchildren's summer visits with us changed from Louisiana to Texas. We enrolled them in summer programs such as tennis, swimming, and field trips to Austin, Houston, and travels to museums sponsored by the College Station ISD. They also visited DeeDee at the Large Animal Medicine and Surgery Department at Texas A&M. He gave them a personal and extended tour of the Large Animal Hospital.

The Texas visits did not quite measure up to their Juanwood experiences because they did not have their Louisiana cousins and other family members to enjoy but met several friends at church and through participating in the summer programs in College Station.

Ross was born in 1991 and missed out on the fun summers with his older siblings, but he had some memorable experiences that Jennifer and Bill did not have. As soon as he was old enough, he came for summer visits to College Station and Kentwood. In 1995, I became a school administrator with a 12 month contract. I was not able to spend weeks in Kentwood during the summer as I had done before with Jennifer and Bill.

I enrolled Ross in Summer Camp with the College Station ISD. Ross went on their out-of-town trip to a water park in Houston. He participated in a two-week baseball camp held at the high school. One day while Derry was working, I took Ross to the Houston Space Museum in southwest Houston. We toured the area outside where we could see the space shuttle. Ross enjoyed activities on the inside such as a space ride.

One Saturday, Derry and I took Ross and a teacher's son to a car track in Houston. Ross drove a car by himself, but the other boy was too small to drive a car so DeeDee drove him. Some afternoons, I took Ross to the Research Park near the Veterinary School to ride his bicycle while we were waiting for DeeDee to join us.

When we made trips back to Louisiana, we enjoyed some great fishing trips with my brother Chuck Wilkes and wife Rebecca who owned a houseboat at Grand Isle. We went fishing in their spacious boat catching various large fish. On one occasion, Aunt Beck allowed Ross to steer the boat to the dock where Uncle Chuck was waiting to load it onto the trailer. One day I took Ross out to the Wilkes farm where he rode his bike around Aunt Faye's house and yard. His bicycle had a flat. Aunt Faye's friend repaired the tire for him so that he could continue riding up and down the road. He rode Aunt Faye's golf cart up to cousin Tam and Luke Brooks' yard to pick blueberries. He swung in the tire swing that has been hanging in the pecan tree in front of the Wilkes house for over fifty years. All of the Wilkes grandchildren, great-grandchildren, and friends have had their pictures taken swinging on this tire swing. Ross was allowed to ride the four-wheeler at Uncle Chuck's farm as long as he did not drive too fast.

Derry was an older man when Ross grew up. Derry was over 60 years of age when Ross came to visit us during the summer. Derry was limited to what he felt like doing in the evenings and on weekends after working long hours at the University and making long drives to and from the prison farms. He did not feel like doing much traveling on the weekends. When we did travel back to Juanwood in Kentwood, Ross enjoyed riding his bike around the yard and in the woods. As he grew older, he drove DeeDee's tractor around Juanwood helping with yard projects.

As a Clinical Associate Professor at the Large Animal Department at the School of Veterinary Medicine at Texas A&M University, some days Derry traveled hundreds of miles carrying students to the various prison farms to practice on the animals. Derry was also Staff Veterinarian for the Texas Department of Corrections which required him to oversee the health and treatment of thousands of beef cattle, hundreds of horses, thousands of swine, hundreds of dogs, etc. on the prison farms throughout the State of Texas.

Following the Lord's Steps

FROM THE TIME DERRY KNEW that he wanted to become a veterinarian and until the time of his death, he was certainly aware of God's plan for his life and knew the Lord had directed his steps. God guided him throughout his years as he raised calves that became a dairy herd requiring the purchase of a dairy farm while he was in high school. This dairy helped finance his college education as he attended pre-veterinary school at LSU and graduating with a Doctor of Veterinary Medicine degree at TAMU in 1958.

Following his graduation, he set up a veterinary practice in Tangipahoa Parish, Louisiana where he was a senior partner owning and operating the Kentwood Veterinary Clinic large-animal practice in Kentwood, LA for 32 years.

After spending these 32 years in practice, he was ready for a greater challenge. He checked into working for the federal government, a primate facility, and looked at other possibilities but nothing happened. He had been contacted by Dr. Allen

Rousell at Texas A&M, asking him to apply for a teaching position at Texas A&M. Derry told him to continue interviewing those candidates who had applied. If a candidate did not accept the position, get back in touch with him. All this time, God was preparing the way for him to join the Texas A&M Veterinary Medicine and Surgery Department as a Clinical Associate professor. In 1990, he accepted the position and spent 17 years teaching and preparing senior veterinary students for practice.

In 1990, I had completed ten years of teaching at Kentwood High School which qualified me to be vested in the Louisiana Retirement System for future retirement benefits. I joined the College Station Independent School District (CSISD) where I spent 17 years teaching and serving in administration. Our professional lives in College Station paralled each other in so many ways making this a great team effort in contributing to the education of veterinary students at TAMU and students in the CSISD. This team effort was carried out in our personal lives as we shared words of our faith and encouragement to people of all walks of life.

Derry had flown to Miami, FL to attend a grandson's football game. On Monday, November 10, 2008, Derry left Miami, after spending time with Steve, Nita and the grandchildren, to begin his flight back to College Station. When he arrived in Houston, he learned that his flight to CS had already taken off. They were able to place him on the next flight which brought him to CS at 8:30 p.m. When he called me from Houston to say that he would be delayed and why, I responded by saying that I would just stay in the airport and wait for him.

A father with his three year old son, sitting across the aisle from me overheard my conversation and stated that I had reacted to the news in such a pleasant way. He was so impressed with my attitude and response to this news that he moved over and sat two seats from me.

We began a long conversation about gardening, politics, religion, and teaching at TAMU. He is a geography professor at TAMU and lives on two acres in Wellborn, growing all kinds of greens that they use to make gumbos, soups, etc. He told me that his son attends Saint Michael's Preschool and is very proud of what he is learning. I asked him if the family attended church, and he stated that they have their own way of worshipping—nature and God's creation. He is Jewish but not a practicing Jew. His parents sent him to the synagogue, but they did not attend. His wife is of another faith.

After the professor's wife arrived and the baggage and waiting area cleared out, another young man sat down across the aisle from me. He was waiting for his fiancée who is working on a PhD in Sociology at TAMU to arrive on the flight that Derry was on. He is an artist but did not complete college because he was not sure what he really wanted to do. Due to lack of funds, he had to drop out of school but was not sure what he wanted to do. He kept talking about how intelligent his fiancée was but did not see himself intelligent enough to complete college. I began to encourage him and reminded him that everyone is gifted and talented. As I assured him that he is smart and could do anything that he wanted to do, I was reminded of the scripture, *"I can do all things through Christ who strengthens me."* Philippians 4:13.

As an encouragement to him, I shared with him on how I had helped my husband receive his Doctor of Veterinary Medicine degree in 1958 from TAMU. After working several years helping Derry in his veterinary practice, I realized that something was missing in my life. I had not reached the highest level of Maslow's Heirarchy of Needs—Self Actualization and wanted to receive a college education.

When my oldest sister lost her husband, the father of her four children, she went to work. I began thinking about not having the means of making a living if something should happen to Derry.

I shared with this young man, "As soon as our only daughter Nita graduated college in 1974, I began my studies at SLU to work on a two-year secretarial degree. I was not sure that I could ever get a four-year college degree. I proved to myself that I could having received my first degree in Business Education in 1978. I continued taking courses receiving two Master's, and a Specialist in Administration and Supervision degree.. After I began teaching in Texas in 1990, I took courses at TAMU and the University of Connecticut to receive my Gift-Talented

Endorsement." I assured this young man that he could do anything that he set his mind to do.

After Derry's plane arrived in CS and we were on our way home from the airport, he told me that he had sat next to a young woman who was working on her Ph.D in Sociology at TAMU. He stated that he told her about me and my years in education.

What a coincidence! Her fiancé visited with me at the airport, and his wife visited with Derry on the plane. In different locations and circumstances we were sharing similar stories to these young adults. Who knows what these experiences will mean to these two young people? We surely did receive a blessing from these visits!

Our Journey Took an Immediate Turn

On Friday, December 30, 2011 was a normal day for Derry and me. We drove to Bryan for me to renew my driver's license which required a long wait. After sitting in the waiting room for quite some time for them to call my name, Derry decided that he would go sit in the van. He was filing his finger nails while waiting patiently for me. We drove to Fish Daddy's to eat fish before going to the Texas A&M Women's Basketball game at Reed Arena on the Texas A&M campus. *"The angel of the Lord encamps around those who fear Him, and delivers them."Psalm 34:7.*

Derry was wearing a back brace to support his back due to a fracture he had obtained when he fell in a boat while fishing in Louisiana in October, 2011. Derry and I chose to sit on the handicapped row at the very top of our seat section where he would have more space to sit and move about. Shortly after half time, Derry was sitting to my right. I said something to him, but he did not respond. He was leaning slightly to the right with his mouth a little drooped. I knew something was wrong. I told the gentlemen sitting next to Derry, "We need help!" He quickly responded by calling for the EMT stationed below in the arena. These *angels* came immediately and began to do what emergency teams do in an emergency situation. Derry was aware enough to try to retrieve the car keys from his pocket for me so that I could follow the ambulance to the hospital.

"For He shall give His angels charge over thee, to keep thee in all thy ways." Psalm 91:11.

We are told that a guardian angel watches over a person from infancy through life. One of God's *angels* administering to Derry that night was Retired Col. Michae Beggs who called for the EMT and stayed with me until Derry left the arena in transport to St. Joseph Hospital. He gave me his card in case I needed to call him.

When I walked out into the arena foyer after the EMT was leaving with Derry, I was surrounded by Christian friends who were at the game and had recognized me and saw that Derry was the reason for the EMT's presence. Our *angels,* former teacher colleague and friend, Pat Norton, and several church friends along with Gene and Zanna Bickham, immediately responded. Pat rode with me to the hospital and her husband Jim and their friends met us at the Hospital. Gene and Zanna Bickham, and other strong Christian friends, were in attendance at the game and met us at the hospital. These Christian friends joined me in the Emergency Waiting Room praying and offering support.

Another *angel* that night on December 30 was Dr. Marcus Purvis, Emergency Medicine Physician, who was on call at the Emergency Room at St. Joseph Hospital in Bryan. Dr. Purvis and his emergency team did some amazing work in treating Derry as his lungs were filling up with fluid. In other words, Derry was literally drowning. The Emergency Team asked me to bring someone in to be with me in case Derry did not survive. So, I asked Gene and Zanna Bickham and Pat Norton to come into the Emergency Room with me where they remained with me at Derry's bedside.

I touched Derry on his shoulder and spoke, "You are going to be fine." Zanna touched his arm and spoke, "You will be fine." Derry shook his head "No." When Zanna and I spoke these words, we were speaking God's words giving us the assurance that Derry was "going to be fine." I asked Gene to pray. As he prayed, we held hands, and we knew that Derry was going to be fine. It is recorded in Isaiah 55:11, *"so is my word that goes out from my mouth; It will not return to me empty, but will accomplish what I desire and achieve the purpose for which I sent it."*

At some point, I called Nita who was in Orlando, FL with her family. She is a nurse who works in the Emergency Room at a hospital in Miami, FL. She asked to talk to Dr. Purvis. After their conversation, he asked me what kind of nursing she did. When I told him emergency room nursing, he said he thought she must have been because of the questions she asked.

Dr. Purvis needed a list of Derry's medications. Because I could not leave Derry, I asked Gene and Zanna Bickham to go to our house and get the notebook from our office that contained the medicine list. There were no outside lights on at the house which made it very difficult for them to see how to find the keyhole to open the door. Zanna parked the car at an angle so that the car lights would provide enough light for Gene to find the keyhole. They successfully returned with the list for Dr. Purvis.

After Derry was stabilizied enough, he was transferred to the Critical Care Unit. Nita called Derry's niece, Dr. Robin Fabre, an internal medicine physician, at Tyler, TX and informed her of Derry's stroke. Robin drove from Tyler Saturday with her husband and daughter's blessings. After Robin and I had returned to our home from the Critical Care Unit, we stood at the kitchen bar praying for her Uncle Derry. Robin, a real prayer warrior, held my hand and prayed fervently for him naming each part of his body.

Saturday, December 31, 2011

"The Lord said to me, 'You have seen correctly, for I am watching to see that my word is fulfilled.'" Jeremiah 1:12.

THE TEAM OF EMERGENCY ROOM DOCTORS, nurses, and other staff members worked diligently and quickly as a team to assess and stabilize Derry. He developed a lot of fluid in his lungs and despite the medical team's interventions he required placement of a breathing tube (intubation) to help him breathe and protect his airway. It was not completely clear at that time what the cause of the fluid in the lungs might have been.

Nita arrived from Orlando, FL on Saturday. These two *angels*, Nita and Robin, remained with me several days. They were so valuable to me and the family having the knowledge and understanding of the medical procedures to write a description of what was going on with Derry on a daily basis. They e-mailed the reports to family and friends keeping everyone informed and up to date.

After all of the testing, it was known that he did have a stroke causing him to have paralysis on the left side of his body. Initially, he was not moving his left lower leg, but later he was able to move it spontaneously. It was determined that he did not have a heart attack nor a blood clot to his lungs, and his heart remained in a normal rhythm. He was placed on IV medications to keep him sedated to allow him to remain on the ventilator to improve his breathing and lung function. His vital signs were very stable. The team was planning to assess his breathing and respiratory status Sunday morning and if all of his parameters look good, then they would try to see if he could be removed off the ventilator. He was responsive when spoken to. The medical staff was very attentive letting us know that this would be a "day by day journey." Their expectation was that he would be in the ICU for 3 to 5 days.

Derry was placed in the Cardiac Intensive Care Unit at St. Joseph Medical Hospital in Bryan. Some friends stopped by the front desk and were told that he was not listed as a patient there. We learned that the receptionist was not looking up the spelling 'Derry Magee' but was using another spelling which caused them to be adamant about his not being a patient there. This issue was resolved. Texans always spelled his last name McGee. Many times we had to spell Magee for them. (Because Derry had to consistently spell his first and last names for receptionists, he had cards printed to show the receptionists who he was and could quickly identify him to obtain his medical records.)

Sunday, January 1, 2012

Derry remained in the Cardiac Intensive Care Unit at St. Joseph Medical Hospital. On this morning, the pulmonologist and respiratory therapists concluded after their evaluation and determined that Derry would tolerate the removal of the endotracheal tube and removal from the ventilator. The IV sedation medications were completed, weaned off as he was following commands well, and able to breathe on his own. He tolerated the removal of the breathing tube very well and kept a good oxygen level all day since its removal.

We found out after speaking to the Cardiologist, Dr. Wiggins, that Derry had had some type of a heart arrhythmia at the time of his stroke and along with the stresses involved with the stroke caused him to develop the "flash pulmonary edema" (fluid in his lungs) that had necessitated the initial placement of the breathing tube. With control of his blood pressure and through the use of other medications, the issue with the pulmonary edema seemed resolved.

Derry was able to recognize all of his visitors and followed commands. By the evening, he really began to look more like the Derry we all know and love. Although, he still had no movement in his left arm, he regained spontaneous and purposeful movement in his left leg. He received nutrition via an oral feeding tube and the following day would receive a full evaluation by the stroke team. The stroke team evaluation would include that of neurology, speech and physical therapy. Additionally, he would have a swallowing evaluation. If he were able to swallow without the risk of aspiration into his lungs, then liquids and eventually solids would be introduced as he was able to tolerate them."

Derry asked every friend who came to see him to pray for him. Derry held out his right hand and gave each visitor a firm handshake. Derry asked one friend who came with three other friends to pray for him. This friend looked at me and whispered, "I don't pray out loud." I asked them to gather around his bed and pray silently for him. The waiting area was filled with colleagues from the LAMS Department at TAMU, family members, and many friends from our church.

Monday, January 2, 2012

Derry remained in the Cardiac Intensive Care Unit at St.Joseph Medical Hospital. He was extubated on Sunday and remained off the ventilator with his oxygen saturations remaining normal with the assistance of oxygen mask.

Overall, he had a very busy day on Monday. He was evaluated by Physical Therapy (PT) in the morning. They were very encouraging with their assessment stating that as soon as the cardiac status permitted, they thought Derry would be a very good candidate for inpatient rehab. He was able to sit on the side of the bed and dangle his legs during the PT assessment with some assistance. The physical therapist stressed that as Derry's stroke on the right side of his brain was causing paralysis on the left arm and what is medically called "left sided neglect" by the brain, we were all encouraged to stimulate him on the left side by approaching the left side of his bed and speaking to him on the left side forcing a "retraining" of the brain to not neglect that portion of his body.

Speech Therapy did a 'bedside' swallowing evaluation and felt that the stroke had affected his gag reflex and ability to swallow without contents going into the lungs so the trial of any kind of liquids was on hold. The staff did state that they are seeing improvement in this area and that they would probably 'test' his swallowing abilities every day or so as they believed he should be able to gain back the ability to swallow.

He had some issues of a very dry mouth and these were addressed with aggressive oral care and placing his oxygen through a water system to "humidify" it so the oxygen would have less of a drying effect. He surely wanted an ice chip, but we had to wait until it was 'safe.' He continued to be alert and able to follow commands. He understood everything that he had heard and cooperated very well with all requests he had been given by his caregivers. He had a mild expressive aphasia where he couldn't quite get out the words he wanted to say but this improved.

Occupational therapy did their evaluation and began exercises specifically targeted at his arms and legs. They were limited in the ferocity of these exercises due to an increase in Derry's heart rate and blood pressure, but they continued to evaluate and treat daily.

The neurologist did her evaluation and gave us very encouraging news. She felt that Derry would recover most if not all of his functions in the course of time barring any other complications. She ordered an MRI of the brain to be performed on Tuesday. She also started a new medication, PLAVIX to help prevent any further extension of his stroke or new ones.

The cardiologist decreased one of the IV medications, amiodarone that was controlling the heart rhythm and started it via the feeding tube route in an attempt to make the conversion from IV to oral for this medication. However, after the neurology evaluation, Derry went back into "atrial fibrillation" with a subsequent increase in his heart rate and blood pressure, so the IV amiodarone dose was increased back again. He remained on a Cardene IV drip to help maintain his blood pressure in an acceptable range.

Derry still had a low grade fever in the 99 F range and remained on the IV antibiotic Levoquin. His white blood count (WBC) was slightly up around 12,000. He did not have a chest x-ray on Monday but would have one on Tuesday, and his urine output remained brisk with his kidney function parameters being normal. We asked everyone to continue praying that Derry would fully recover.

Tuesday, January 3, 2012

Derry's niece, Dr. Robin Fabre, who had been at the hospital providing support for us, left College Station and traveled to Ponchatoula, LA to accompany her mother on a doctor's visit Wednesday. We really missed her, but we had to share her. Nita calls her the traveling doctor now.

When I called Nita on Friday night after Derry's stroke to notify her about her Daddy, Nita thought for a moment about whom she could contact to assist me with any interpretations, thoughts, explanations, etc. while she was traveling from Orlando, FL. Robin's name immediately popped into her head.

Robin was such a blessing to us. She shared her time, spiritual strengths, prayers, and medical knowledge during these critical hours and days. We appreciated her family for their support and patience as she traveled to College Station to be with us.

I remained at home Tuesday morning to do household chores, return phone calls, call dear friends and families, and take care of business. Nita visited her daddy during the morning visiting hours. Nita and I met my nephew Patrick Schilling at Must Be Heaven for lunch.

Derry's heart rate and blood pressure became more controlled. The Neurologist ordered an MRI of the brain. However, the unhappy news was that it showed bleeding in the area of the ischemic stroke (this is medically termed as a hemorrhagic conversion). The neurologist ordered a stat CAT scan of the brain to further evaluate the area and size of the bleed. The Plavix was immediately withheld.

The hospitalist came during Tuesday evening visiting hours to report to us the results of the CAT scan of the brain. I asked him, "Is he going to make it?" He shook his head, "No." I responded, "Doctor, we are Christians and believe that Derry will be healed." In 2 Corinthians 4:13 it reads: *"It is written: 'I believed; therefore I have spoken.' Since we have that same spirit of faith, we also believe and therefore speak."*

At the afternoon visiting session from 5:30 p.m. to 6:00 p.m., Derry had difficulty opening his eyes and was very tired. He continued to have the same strength in his right hand, leg and left foot. Two of Derry's colleagues went back to speak to Derry, and he responded with nods but had difficulty opening his eyes. We were all a little disappointed but continued to remain positive. Derry and Dora's pastor Rev. Troy Allen surprised all of us with a visit. He ended his 6:00 p.m. visit with us in prayer.

We waited patiently to hear from the Neurologist with her interpretation of the CAT scan results and her evaluation of Derry. We missed her, so the nurse called her. We were informed that after her review of the CAT scan and evaluation of Derry, she felt that things were "status quo" and she added two new medications-one to aid the heart and one to protect the brain from developing spasms (Brain attacks-seizures). The Amiodarone was lowered further, and Derry tolerated the lower dose well. His heart rate and blood pressure during the night were well controlled.

During the 8:00 p.m. to 9:00 p.m. visit, Nita was talking to Derry about his grandchildren and the extended members of the family. He gave a HIGH thumbs-up to Chase for taking his first step. He was pleased to hear about Mia, "the Duck lady" as she was the Duck Master at the Peabody Hotel on Sunday evening. She escorted the ducks out of the pond, into the elevator, and up to the Penthouse. The Nebraskan football team and tons of fans were present for the ceremonies. Nita told Derry about grandson Bill's father-in-law who fell leaving the hotel on Monday morning and stated that the only thing that did not hurt were his feet. The father-in-law was doing well within a few days. Our granddaughter Jennifer called, and Derry was asked if he would be able to hear Jennifer talk to him. He shook his head "no," so she sent a message telling him goodbye. Derry promptly lifted his right arm high in the air waving "goodbye" to her. At the end of visiting hours, we told him goodnight. He responded with a squeeze of his hand.

We were patiently taking Derry's progress a half day at a time. Nita told him that the doctors were having a little trouble with his brain and asked him to say a prayer to Jesus for himself. He responded with a nod.

Pain is not something anyone wishes on anyone else, but we were very happy that Derry could tell us where his back hurt by lifting his right leg and hip and placing his right hand on the area.

We gave Nita's family an update on the day's happenings and confirmed that Robin had made it safely to her destination.

In our e-mail at the end of the day, Nita and I signed off with a special 'thank you' to all who had been sharing their time and prayers with us.

Wednesday, January 4, 2012

This day was an informative one for us as Derry's regular doctors returned to duty after the holidays. We learned explicitly from Derry's cardiologist that Derry had not thrown a blood clot caused by Atrial Fib. In 1935, Derry had a baby brother who bled to death. The family history of bleeding could possibly be attributed to Von Willebrand's Disease. Derry's other sibling was diagnosed with VonWillebrand's disease. Derry had never been tested for Von Willebrand's, but the doctors felt that this could have been a contributing cause to his propensity for bleeding. A repeat CT scan was done to evaluate for further changes. At this time, we did not have all the results.

Two of Derry's close friends came to see him. After acknowledging their presence, Derry motioned for one of them to come over and pray for him, and this friend did. He then motioned for the other friend to come over, and he held his hand and they prayed.

During the 5:30 p.m. visitation, Derry stated that he wanted a bath. He had been bathed that morning when PT had him standing during therapy. But, Nita and I quickly agreed to give him another bath. While we were bathing him, he took the wash cloth from my hands and began washing his hair. He asked for another wash cloth. I gave him a clean dry one. He told me that he wanted water on it. I asked if he wanted cold or hot water. He stated, 'cold.' He took the wash cloth and wiped his left eye which had a cream in it to keep the eye moist. He pulled up the oxygen mask and wiped out the inside of his lips and mouth. Because Derry was not able to swallow, Dr. Ragu inserted a PEG for his feeding.

Derry's speech showed some improvement. We were able to understand more of his speech. Nita showed him a holiday card that our neighbor girl had drawn. Her holiday card won the art contest last year at her elementary school. When he saw the card, he grabbed it from Nita's hand and looked at it. Nita also showed him pictures of his great-grandchildren which he enjoyed. The next day, we took his glasses to him so that he could see the pictures better. Grandson Bill told us that Kellye had mailed a card that great-grandchildren "Mia and Chase" made for Dee Dee. Derry looked forward to receiving it.

Nita and I were comforted by hearing a nun read the 23rd Psalms on the intercom. We took Derry's Bible on Thursday and read this Psalm to him.

As we all know, life is a journey. We think we are headed in one direction but can suddenly be taken in another. Our family has a tremendous faith in Christ, and we know that our journey through life is guided through Him. Our faith is tested constantly, and we are tested constantly. We will continue to trust in the guiding hand of Christ through our journey. Derry has been a true guiding force for our family to which we are all thankful.

Again, as we signed off tonight, we thanked everyone for their prayers and asked for very specific prayers now for Derry's healing. Robin, our niece and cousin, has been praying very specifically for her "Uncle Derry," praying over every part of his body as only a medical doctor could do.

Thursday, January 5, 2012

Prayer brought further improvement. Derry was stronger. He could turn himself to his left with minimal assistance. Plans were made for Derry to be transferred to the Stroke/Telemetry area at St. Joseph Hospital sometime Friday. The Physical, Occupational, and Speech Therapy teams worked with Derry every morning. With him being out of the ICU, the teams were able to increase his therapy. He participated in everything he was asked to do. He did not get frustrated or show anger. We looked forward to receiving more information about Derry's further care.

Derry really brightened up when Nita told him that our grandson Bill and wife Kellye Johnson, would be traveling from Nashville, TN and arriving in College Station on Saturday morning, January 7.

Friday, January 6, 2012

Today in Nita's e-mail report to family and friends, she referred to Derry as Daddy and referred to me as Mom. Nita wrote, "Daddy asked Mom to stay with him tonight so she did. Daddy was moved from ICU last night to Telemetry floor, Room

201. He completed physical therapy this morning with a few steps with assistance and the walker. Of course, he was extremely tired after the work out, but we were very encouraged."

"Accomplishments for my Dad have changed. A giant step for you or me would be an infant step for my Dad. So we were just as excited at his infant accomplishments as a parent would have been with a child who took his or her first step."

"I was able to observe Occupational Therapy today and learn some of the exercises that Mom and I can help support. One thing the medical staff asked was that everyone who visits him should go around to his left side. He needed to exercise turning to his left side. This afternoon, he started moving his left leg up and down slowly without being prompted. Daddy's speech has improved more from yesterday."

"Daddy received a card today from a group. Please forgive me for not remembering which one. He put on his glasses to read the card, but we had brought the wrong glasses. We have since remedied that, so we will now be reading cards and looking at pictures of grandkids and great grand kids."

"His older grandson Bill and wife Kellye are currently driving in tonight from Nashville and will be visiting tomorrow. My cousin Patrick, his wife, and three children plan to come tomorrow. I told Daddy that we would be bothering him all day. His response was, 'THAT'S GREAT!'"

In our nightly e-mails to family and friends, Nita and I asked everyone to please continue to come by for visits. Visits brighten his spirit and encourage him. We thanked them for their continued prayers and words of encouragement.

Sunday, January 8, 2012

Bill and Kellye made a safe journey back to Nashville, TN, and Nita made a safe flight back to Miami. Nita returned to her work at the Veterans Administration Hospital in Miami this morning. I learned this week that rather than calling someone to find out which channel would televise the LSU-Alabama football game, I should have asked Derry. He knew the channel number; he also knew the best route for Bill and Kellye to travel returning to Nashville, plus he listened to everything we said and corrected us when we were mistakened. This was how we knew that his mind was 100% with us. The swallowing improved and the other parts of his body were being restored gradually.

Dr. Gene King who is over 90 years of age had become a coffee buddy to Derry and the McDonald's Coffee Club group. Dr. King came to the hospital Sunday afternoon with his cane and walked the long hallways accompanied by his caregiver. . Several family members were waiting to go in to see Derry, but I asked the family to allow Dr. King to go in ahead of them, and they did. When I met him in the hallway, he stated, "I have come to see if my prayers are working." I assured him that they were working. He walked into Derry's room, spoke to him, and shook his hand. He stated, "Yes, my prayers are working." He and his caregiver left the room and walked down the long hallway to return home

God poured out so many blessings on Derry and our family. Derry has always had such a brilliant mind and always used it in a purposeful way. The amazing thing about his stroke is that it did not affect his mind. He knew everybody who came to see him and called them by name. He was very observant of things around him and was aware of what was going on with his body.

Monday, January 9, 2012

I informed family and friends that I would not be sending daily updates on Derry's progress because my medical writers, Nita and Robin, had returned to their homes. I told them that I would be sending communications periodically.

Because Derry was doing extremely well, all parties involved in his medical care met and made the decision to transfer him to the St. Joseph Rehab at 1600 Joseph Drive, Bryan, Texas 77802. While Dr. James Bonds, primary physician, was making his rounds in the hospital, he came by and stated that Derry would be transported to Rehab by 10:00 a.m. The ambulance team was standing at Derry's door a few minutes before 10:00 a.m. As soon as the ambulance left with Derry, I immediately began removing items from the room. I followed the Rehab van to the Rehab facility which is only a few blocks from the main hospital. I remained with Derry while they gathered information. As they began to assess and perform therapy, I went home to unload things. I returned to the Rehab around 5:00 p.m. and remained until 8:30 a.m. the next morning. I had a cot in a small room next to his room. When the staff came to treat him, feed him, and perform therapies, I went home to bathe and take care of things in our home. He had several visitors during the afternoon.

To avoid any unnecessary trips down a long hallway, I sent a short report letting everyone know that he was in Room 118 at the St. Joseph Rehab.

Derry was a testimony to the power of God and what He can do for us. I asked everyone to continue praying for him as the therapist worked on his swallowing so that he could eat regular food. Those who knew him knew how much he liked to eat. He was not hungry because he was being fed through the PEG— stomach tube. He was in Rehab on Tuesday from around 8:00-12:00 noon. Our primary goal in the rehabilitating process was for Derry to be able to return to our home as soon as possible."

Saturday, January 14, 2012

Derry made great strides in his swallowing. During speech therapy on Friday, Derry was given to eat ground fish, mixed vegetables, apple nectar, and chocolate pudding. The first thing he told me when I arrived was what he had eaten, and he liked it. Upon my arrival in the afternoon, he happened to notice that I had Blue Bell ice cream in my lunch. Derry immediately wanted some. At this point, no one could feed him but the speech therapists. I asked his therapist, Nancee Dixon, who came down to his room and personally fed him a cup of vanilla ice cream. Water flows faster through the throat and causes a greater risk of water going down into the lungs. The nectar flows smoother and slower and goes down the esophagus better. It was a thrilling sight watching Derry hold his cup and drink for himself.

Last night, the nurse removed the triple line from his upper right chest area where the medications were being given. Since he was able to swallow crushed pills in the nectar, it was time to remove the port. They also administered the crushed pills through the stomach tube and continued to do so until he was able to eat enough calories to sustain him. He only had two tubes left to be removed— the catheter and the feeding tube

He thoroughly enjoyed ALL visitors. They stimulated him and kept him aware of everything that was going on. Derry felt very much a part of what was going on in the lives of people, TAMU School of Veterinary Medicine, First Baptist Church of CS, football, basketball, politics, friends, and family. He was so disappointed in LSU not showing up for the game. He had a lengthy conversation with Steve, our son-in-law in Miami, about football. Derry kept repeating, "Jefferson is no quarterback." "Jefferson is no quarterback." I thought, "What a shame the LSU coach did not know that!" Derry and others felt that the coach should have replaced him with Lee after the first fumble."

Derry asked Patrick to bring his daughter Kathryn by to see him on their way from daycare. Pat brought her by last Tuesday and Patrick, Jennifer, Conner, David, and Kathryn visited him that afternoon. One door in his room was covered with artwork done by our neighbors, Noura and Sara, Connor and David Schilling, and great-granddaughter Mia Johnson from Nashville, TN.

Derry told his nurse that when he got well he would like to teach the physical therapists human anatomy so that they would know the proper way to sit a male during showers. If you knew Derry, he always told it like it was!

Because Derry was cold in Rehab, Sandra and Gerald Wynn, two of the truest and greatest friends anyone could have, went to our house, picked up Derry's warm long knit shirts and brought them to Rehab. They took his new shirts and putter pant bottoms to wash for his use in Rehab.

Derry's first cousin, Dr. Charles Bridges, passed away Thursday morning. Derry asked me to attend the wake. I thought that I would, but I was too exhausted to prepare to attend the wake at night. Walking down the long halls at St. Joseph several times a day was very exhausting.

Wednesday, January 18, 2012

Our family praised God daily for Derry's progress! Each Tuesday, the St. Joseph Rehab team met, reported progress, and made recommendations for the next steps in Derry's rehabilitation. On Tuesday, January 24, we would have an idea of when he would be discharged from St. Joseph Rehab to a Skilled Nursing facility.

The hospital bed at the Rehab was too small for his body. Upon my request, they ordered a large bed for him. It turned out to be a large wide bed which was very difficult to push down the carpeted hallways to the cafeteria. The staff did not want him to remain in his room to eat; therefore, I had to push this large heavy bed to and from the cafeteria. Their expectation was that I would push him which was very difficult for me.

I was able to rest comfortably in the small private room in his suite which had a lavatory and a cot. While Derry was receiving PT, OT, and Speech therapies during the day at the Rehab, I used this time to go home to bathe, dress, do house chores, and take care of business. I ordered supper from the cafeteria and ate with Derry in the dining area which had large open windows overlooking the trees.

Having family, friends and neighbors looking after things around the house was very helpful and comforting. Our nephew Patrick Schilling and his family filled the bird feeders and water container for the birds, cranked Derry's truck, ran errands, pruned plants, etc. The Hilal's put out the garbage can for pick-up and returned it to the rear of the house. They were good neighbors who did many things to help.

Several months ago, our son-in-law, Steve Johnson's Aunt Kitty Kane (Aunt Mina) called and invited me to be her guest at the College Station Christian Women's luncheon and style show at Pebble Creek Country Club on Tuesday, January 17. Aunt Mina gave her Christian testimony, and I was so glad that I had made the decision to attend. She is a writer, speaker, vocalist, song writer, and a strong Christian who lives in Arlington, TX. After we returned from the luncheon, we went to the St. Joseph Rehab to visit Derry. Derry was so pleased that I had attended the luncheon and was extremely pleased to see Aunt Mina. I knew a large number of the members attending the luncheon and decided to join this group which is affiliated with the Stonecroft Ministries. When my longtime friend Velta Morris from S. C. learned that I would be attending, she stated, "Dora, you are made for this organization."

In an e-mail to family and friends, I expressed to them how blessed Derry and I were by the way they showed Godly love to us. They ministered to Derry in numerous ways when they visited him.

Derry's niece, Dr. Robin Fabre, from Tyler called us Tuesday afternoon and stated that she was coming Thursday afternoon to spend three nights with her Uncle Derry at the St. Joseph Rehab and to give me a rest. Jimmie Lard came one morning while I was at home and helped me take down the Christmas decorations. She also cleaned the newly renovated shower and had it ready for Derry to use. *What a gift!*

Thursday, January 26

The day finally came for Derry to leave the St. Joseph Rehab and move to a skilled nursing facility at the Isle at Watercrest. He was placed in Room 314 which had a bed that was too small for him. His feet pressed against the bottom of the bed. I immediately requested a longer bed.

Friday, January 27

Derry worked very hard in rehab even though it was a struggle. Physical therapists were amazed at Derry's determination and strong will to recover. The therapists applied electrical stimulation on his left side. The Speech therapist used Vital Stem Therapy on his throat which increased his ability to chew and swallow. He successfully swallowed ten sips of water on Friday without aspirating. Occupational therapists worked on training him to do personal daily tasks. His cognitive ability and memory were incredible. Sequencing was one area that stroke patients find difficult, but Derry could tell the speech therapist every step used in driving his truck, beginning with getting the keys off the key ring and remembering to raise the garage door.

One interesting observation was when the OT was teaching Derry how to wash his hands, Derry washed and dried his right hand. The OT asked him if he had another hand. He picked up his left hand with his right hand and carefully washed and dried it. He never forgot to include the left hand. When the body's left side is affected by a stroke, the patient does not see his left side. This also affected his inability to read at this time. As the left side recovered, he became more conscious that there was something to his left. This was why we asked visitors to always go to his left side to force him to look to the left.

Saturday, January 28, 2012

After Derry had been transferred to his wheelchair, his left arm began to shake for a second. I wondered if he were having some kind of attack. I also became excited that his left side might be "waking up." One family member thought perhaps it could have been a seizure since he was administered seizure medicine when at St. Joseph Hospital earlier.

At some point Saturday, I observed Derry lying in bed holding his left hand with his right and massaging the left hand and arm with eyes closed. The speech therapist had shared with Derry and me some results of a research that used the MRI on three occasions to show how the brain was able to become activated when the patient imagined doing a task. In the first MRI, the patient was asked to do nothing during the hour. During the second MRI, the patient was instructed to continuously do a task during the hour (saying a word or moving a finger, etc). During the third task, the patient was asked to only think about doing the task that he performed in the second MRI. At the end of the third MRI, they found that the brain responded the same way as it had when the patient performed the task during the second MRI.

"It was a miracle"

Sunday, January 29, 2012

As Derry was massaging the hand with his eyes closed, I was sure he was praying. He told everyone that God was healing his left side. His words were, "It is a miracle."

After lunch on Sunday, Derry was lying in bed when all of a sudden his left foot and ankle began to move. He called me and excitingly stated, "Dora, look at my left foot!" It was moving back and forth. I ran over to him in the bed. We embraced, cried, and thanked Jesus for this healing. We immediately began to call our family members to tell them the good news. Derry was so emotionally moved that he could not to talk. I talked to our family members crying tears of joy. Later Derry called them and was able to talk. As word spread throughout the Isle at Watercrest on Sunday afternoon among the nurses, aides, assistants, and the Director of Nursing, they all came to see what had happened. They were very moved with tears. Many believed from the beginning that Derry would be healed because of his strong faith in God. One aide stated, "I knew that he would be healed because he asked us each morning at 7:00 a.m. to turn on his TV to Channel 14 so that he could hear Chris Osborne's sermons, "Verse by Verse." He plays one of his favorite CD piano hymns during the day and in the evening while he is sleeping.

Derry was very excited when our pastor, Rev. Troy Allen and his family, came Saturday afternoon to visit. His children brought get well cards that they had made which were added to his card collection. Troy's sermons are on line now. We were also very blessed to have our niece Jennifer, Conner, Kathryn, and friends Gerald and Sandra who came for a visit.

Every day, he had faithful visitors who came to pray with him, encourage him, read books to him, and help him with his I-Pad. Dr. Steve Wikse, a former colleague from the LAMS Department at the TAMU School of Veterinary Medicine, continued to remain committed coming to read and discuss veterinary articles and other interesting topics with Derry. Steve ministered to Derry through these readings and discussions that were mentally stimulating. Other veterinarians came to visit and shared common experiences in their veterinary practices. Steve's wife Bonnie came to visit when her schedule allowed.

Tuesday, February 7, 2012

Derry's McDonald's Coffee Club buddies came to visit him at the Isle. The Isle served them an array of goodies in the Club Room. Tom Gibbs brought Dr. Gene King, age 94, to visit. Dr. King and Derry had a very special relationship.

. Several SS friends came during the weekend bringing book CD's for him. He and I listened to three CD's from Tom Brokaw's book. We listened to the Rick Warren's CD from one of his books. I brought Derry a large vase of red roses.

Longtime friends, Dick and Libby Day from Shreveport, La., came to visit. They joined us for lunch in the private dining room at the Isle. They helped set-up Derry's I-Pad. That evening Dick did some clean-up work on our home computer. They learned about the I-Pad through an e-mail and knew how to help.

Also, a week later, Mike Beggs and his wife came to visit. Mike gave Derry some pointers on the use of the I-Pad while I had a delightful visit with his wife. They were two of our "angels" at Reed Arena the night Derry had his stroke. We will always be grateful to them for knowing what to do.

February 15-19, 2012

Derry and I were so blessed to have our daughter, Juanita Johnson (Nita) from Miami, FL, spend a few days with us. She was to have arrived at Easterwood Airport on Wednesday evening at 10:45. I managed to drive to the airport in one of the most dangerous fog situations that I have ever experienced when going to pick up her. We waited several minutes for the plane to land, but we received a message that the plane had circled over CS for about 30 minutes trying to land.

Because of the dense fog, the pilot could not see the lights on the runway to safely land. They returned to the Houston airport and passengers were made to believe that there might be another late night flight to CS, but that did not happen. Nita tried to get a hotel room but without success. At 2:15 a.m., she decided to make a bed on the seats in the baggage area and got a few hours of sleep before the first flight out on Thursday morning at 10:30 a.m. She was able to arrive in CS at 11:45 a.m. and was in her dad's room by 12:30 p.m. After the long delay in finally arriving in College Station, she only missed 3-4 hours being with her dad.

Nita is a registered nurse and spent the four days literally taking care of her daddy. She attended his therapy classes and assisted with transitions from the bed to the wheelchair and from the wheelchair to other locations. Nita was truly amazed at her dad's progress. Someone asked her what she thought about his progress. She stated, "I am pleased 100%." She engaged him in some therapy exercises during times when he was not in therapy. She even had him practicing facial exercises while waiting for our lunches. She wheeled him down to the first floor for lunch three days in the beautiful spacious dining room which had lots of windows.

Thursday, February 16, 2012

Approximately, 20 members of the Louis Bonds Men's SS class came for a visit. The Isle staff prepared desserts, coffee, and punch in the large dining room. Derry had a great love and respect for these men whom he had known for over 20 years. Three of the wives came who have been church friends of mine for 20 years. Nita enjoyed being with these friends whom she has met from time to time.

Friday, February 17, 2012

Nita pushed Derry in the First Heart Walk at IAW. She pushed him in the wheelchair around the perimeter of the IAW campus. I followed behind with Cindy the activities director who was walking Dr. Turner's dog, Zora. It was a fun time for everyone. Many residents from the other Watercrest buildings participated in the Heart Walk. On Saturday afternoon, Nita took her daddy for another wheelchair stroll on the sidewalks around the Watercrest campus. The weather was cool, but Derry enjoyed the outings being pushed by his daughter. He loved every minute being with her. After she left to go back to Miami, he looked at me and stated, "She is tough!" I told him that she put him through the extra therapy sessions because she loved him and wanted him to fully recover. She was very pleased as she flew back to Miami on Sunday. Praise God! She did not have any glitches in her flight home.

We are so blessed to be in the facility whose administrator, David Armand, expected his staff to provide the very best care for the IAW's residents. Derry's speech therapist, Jane Colbert, did an incredible job in helping him rehabilitate his chewing and swallowing through the use of the Vital Stem Therapy. She also taught us so much about how the stroke affects victims and the importance of therapies for them. She continually cited research studies on strokes.

Jane reported that Derry was doing well with a regular diet and could independently tell you what strategies were used for swallowing safely. Because water travels so fast when swallowed, it is usually the last beverage a stroke victim can swallow successfully. He continued to take his pills with thickened liquids but drank water in small sips throughout the day. As he was successfully swallowing water, they reduced the amount of water in the feeding tube. Because his appetite was back to normal eating regular food, Dr. Turner stopped the midnight feeding tube.

February 22, 2012

Derry's weight was 222 lbs. which was a gain of 6 ounces for the week. Doctors did not want him to gain back the 30+ pounds he had lost since the stroke. Derry continued the Shaker exercises which was a part of his home program (facial massage, the Elvis snarl, and smile on left side). His cognition was excellent as he read ads and answered correctly 14/15 questions from an exercise. He could do problem-solving activities with no cues. Peripheral vision was affected on the left side which is why visitors were asked to go to his left side to force him to use that side for vision. Scanning was a very important skill for him to have when he began walking independently.

Bridget, his occupational therapist, was so pleased with his progress. He performed all grooming procedures independently. He made a transfer by standing and pivoting with moderate assist

(50% self and 50% assist). He lifted his left leg up on the therapy bed from the floor with 50% assist from OT. He made more left finger extinctions and wrist movement. He did five to 20 reps with each muscle in his arms.

Alicia, the physical therapist, assisted by intern Sylwva, put him on the Nu-Step for the first time on Monday. He averaged making 73 repetitions per minute during ten minutes on the machine. At the end of 10 minutes, he asked for water. He then asked if he could do five more repetitions because the exercise felt good to his left thigh. He felt that this activity was strengthening his legs. He could now stand with minimal assistance.

We were told on Wednesday by the therapists that their goal for him was to walk out on his own from the Isle at Watercrest. He told them that he was in no hurry to leave IAW because he liked the facility, the administration, staff, and therapists.

Many of you were concerned about my well-being. I am doing beautifully. I went to IAW around 10:00 a.m. and returned home around 5:30 p.m. After returning home, I prepared our income tax return, maintained the home, and kept up with the mail and business transactions. I attended the B/CS Christian Women's luncheon at Pebble Creek Country Club on Tuesday and enjoyed the fellowship of Christian ladies from my church and community.

February 23, 2012

I went to the Isle early to have lunch with Derry in the large dining room downstairs. The weather was warm which allowed us to take a "short" stroll outside. He enjoyed being outside. As he recovered, he became very appreciative of the love, prayers, and visits from family and friends, he wrote this letter of "Reflections."

Derry's Letter of Reflections

DERRY'S REFLECTIONS TO THE CORNERSTONE CLASS, Men's Class, Winsome Class, and LAMS Department at TAMU on July 12, 2012

"When I reflect on where I was on December 30, 2011 and where I am now, I know that it is truly an example of God's healing power and the prayers of this Cornerstone Class, a couples Sunday Class at First Baptist Church of College Station taught by Dr. Elvin Smith. Many people might not know that there are angels in our midst and in this Cornerstone Class, but we have personally experienced the manifestations of the angel power."

"On December 30, 2011 at Reed Arena when I had the stroke, we were surrounded immediately by fellow Christians, friends, and members of this class. Some of you came to be with us at the St. Joseph Emergency Room, prayed with us, and remained with Dora until I was moved to the CCU. This class was faithful to continue visiting me and praying with Dora and me in the St. Joseph CCU, ICU, St. Joseph Rehab, and the Isles at Watercrest."

"On March 31, Dora fractured her sacroiliac and her lumbar 1 as she lifted a very heavy item gathering things from my room at the Isles to bring home. Good friends, Sandra and Gerald Wynn, accompanied her to the emergency room and later doctor visits. She was unable to stand or walk for six weeks but was free of pain as long as she lay flat on her back. Sandra came to our home each day to check on her and left prepared food in the refrigerator. She also took yogurt to Derry who remained in the Isle at Watercrest. Another good friend, Judy Sanders, shopped for groceries and put them in the refrigerator. Dora took meals from the refrigerator quickly and rushed back to the bedroom where she ate her meals on a tray lying on her side in the bed. We were blessed to have my niece, Dr. Robin Fabre, from Tyler to help us a few days until Nita and Steve arrived from Miami."

"We think that these six weeks of bed rest allowed the fractures healing time because now she is up and doing almost anything that she wants to do. She is careful not to lift anything over 10 lbs. and has been cautioned by her doctors not to fall under any circumstances. If anything positive came from this experience, it was her weight loss of approximately 20 pounds."

"I walked out of the Isles on my own and came home the middle of April, 2012, with the assistance of good friends Gerald and Sandra Wynn and nephew Patrick Schilling to begin the transition from the Isles at Watercrest to our home where Traditions Home Health began care of my medical and physical needs, providing occupational therapies at home. We immediately engaged the services of Comfort Keepers who provided caregivers daily seven days a week for Dora and me. Dora and I have begun out-patient therapies at the CS Medical Center."

"As soon as we were settled at home, you continued to pray, visit, and telephone daily to see if we needed anything. Many of you were always there for Dora when she needed someone to take her to a doctor's appointment. We could not have made it through these seven months without Christian friends and family like you." *Derry*

*God sends us friends and family
to bless us every day.
Their loving ways etch in our heart
and never fade away.* By Rosemary Nelson

Velta and Bill Morris.

The Bill Morris family.

When we lived in Kentwood, La for 32 years, we were blessed to have Bill and Velta Morris as our close Christian friends. They provided great support for us and our daughter. We shared many meals together and always enjoyed the Christian fellowship with them and their sons, Art and Andy Morris. There was nothing that they would not do for us or anyone in our community. We missed them greatly after they moved to South Carolina where they live today.

When Derry and I moved to College Station, we met Gerald and Sandra Wynn and became good friends. Gerald was my principal at Oakwood and Sandra was a second grade teacher at Rock Prairie Elementary. Sandra and I met for lunch during our Christmas school break our first Christmas that we were in CS. We learned that we both had September birthdays and a love for quilts and antiques. After a week of teaching, the four of us ate at some of our favorite restaurants on Friday nights. Sandra and I visited antique shops and other businesses on Saturdays or during our school holidays.

Gerald and Sandra with family after Texas A&M graduation ceremonies.

Sandra and Gerald were always there to help us with anything that we needed. While Derry was in the Isle, Sandra came to my rescue when my "energy efficient Elite Sears Kenmore washer" failed to successfully spin out the water. After struggling with it for over an hour, I called Sandra. She came over and picked up the wet towels and sheets and completed the laundry. Derry and I had been struggling with the inefficiency of this "elite" washer for quite some time. In 2006, this washer was Sears latest model and the selling point was that it did not have a dasher. That washer ruined two good sets of sheets that got caught under the center part of the washer and ripped 12-15 inches in the sheets. It cut holes in several pieces of clothing. When I told Derry about the newest struggles trying to wash clothes, he quickly replied, "Go buy a new one." The next morning I went to Lowe's and researched washers. I immediately made the decision to get a Maytag washer with a dasher that did a better job than the "expensive paper weight washer" that went to recycling.

Gwendora Magee

JOURNALS

Journal April 9, 2013

Approximately a year ago, Derry returned home after 3 ½ months in the hospital, rehab, and skilled nursing facility from the stroke on December 30, 2011. He is recovering beautifully due to his determination and the healing power of our Lord. He attends occupational therapy once a week to help him regain complete use of his left arm and hand.

As we both began to recover, we reduced the caregivers to five hours a day seven days a week and eventually eliminated their services on the weekends. Even though our long term care insurance pays for the five hours a day seven days a week, we just needed some time to ourselves. Derry and I have learned to manage without the help on the weekend. We have also cut back on the daily hours to three hours daily. On some Saturdays when Alex, a TAMU college student, is available, we have him do special things for Derry, such as; cleaning his guns, doing projects in the yard, picking up grocery items that are too heavy for us to lift, installing a new laser printer, installing a microphone for Derry's Dragon Speak to Write program, etc.

Since we have completed writing our book and submitted it for publication, Derry hopes now to do some medical writing with this new program Dragon, since he does not have good use of his left hand yet.

We traveled to Louisiana in October to be with the family during the Washington Parish Free Fair. Fair time in October has become a family reunion for us as we gather in Jan's yard and outside "playhouse" next to the fairground. Our grandson Ross Johnson flew from Miami to College Station to spend several days with us. He was our chauffer on the trip to and from Louisiana. He is an excellent driver and drove the speed limit that we like to travel due to our "ages." He was able to spend time with many of his cousins, and they got to know him.

In order to help Derry maintain good health, we begin the mornings around 6:00 a.m. by taking his glucose level, blood pressure, and weight. He prepares his instant oatmeal to eat while taking his medications. We prepare all meals at home eliminating salt, some fats, sugar, and seeds. He still uses the thickening in a diet cranberry juice when taking his medications. He eats baked fish twice daily, steamed broccoli, cauliflower, and green beans. I make him desserts without the forbidden ingredients. In fact, we found some strawberries at SAM'S large enough for me to peel for him to eat. I boiled the peels and seeds, ran them through the food processor and strained them through a cheese cloth. I added this juice to a sugar free cobbler which contained frozen pears and diced prunes. He loved it. I try to keep a sweet potato or pumpkin pie baked and ready to eat. This gives him a vegetable in dessert form.

We have become fairly independent with me driving us to the grocery, doctor appointments, therapy, Wellness Center for weight bearing exercises, and other excursions. We are very self-sufficient in ordering medications and organizing them for consumption.

Derry has been trying to grow a particular vine that grows in our neighbor's yard which the birds love because of the purple berries it produces. Last year, we dug up a sprout from the root of the vine and transplanted it in the edge of the neighbors' lot next door but did not have any success. We also scattered some of the berries around hoping that they would sprout. To our surprise, as we were preparing the ground to transplant some vine seedlings, we noticed a vine sprout growing where we were preparing to plant our small plants. Evidently, it came up from one of the seeds sown last year.

In order to make room for this vine bed in the vacant lot next door, we had to cut back a small tree, some underbrush, and roots. Derry took these cut branches to the front of our property for trash pick-up on Monday. He was walking briskly back to where I was so that he could sit and rest. He missed the chair and tumbled over on his left side in the grass. We were instructed to call 911 if he ever fell.

But we activated our plan for helping him up when this happens. I pulled a chair next to him and sat stabilizing my chair with my weight. (Because of my fractured back, I am never to pull on him.) This allowed him to pull himself up by his right hand and arm. When it was all over, we just sat and laughed and continued with our vine bed. He was so thrilled that we had completed a project that he had so long wanted to do.

Salma, our neighbor, says, "Dr. Derry feeds the birds and we have the birds in our yard." Derry is hoping to get some of those birds in his yard so that he can enjoy hearing and watching them. He is watching a chickadee as she builds her nest in the bluebird house on the back fence.

We attend church and Sunday school each week, J.O.Y luncheon for senior adults at the beginning of each month, and Hamburger Night with six other couples from our church and SS. Upon invitations, we attend all functions at the College of Veterinary Medicine at TAMU.

On Wednesday, we met with an attorney who had prepared legal forms for us to sign naming our Medical Power of Attorney, HIPAA Release and Authorization, and Directive to Physicians and Family Surrogates. We delivered copies to our daughter, primary physicians, and the CS Medical Hospital. Got that done! Whew!

We were so blessed to have our entire family (ten members) at Christmas with us in College Station. Steve, Nita, Jennifer, and Ross with their three dogs drove from Miami. Bill and Kellye drove from Nashville, TN with their children Mia and Chase. We had three busy and glorious days together.

On Christmas Day, we ate at the Hilton Christmas Buffet which the family enjoyed. The most wonderful thing about doing something like this, we did not have to spend two days preparing the food and hours cleaning the kitchen. Christmas evening, Patrick, Jennifer, Conner, David and Kathryn joined our family for dinner at our home for potluck. Before leaving for Louisiana, Ross and Steve finished the flag pole and mounted the flag which is flying constantly in our back yard.

Our Wilkes family had a reunion on December 29 at Craig and Pam Forrest's home near Kentwood, La. Craig, Trent and others roasted a pig which was enjoyed by everyone. Side dishes were provided by the Wilkes grandchildren and others. Steve, Nita, Jennifer, and Ross delayed their trip back to Miami a day so that they could attend and see everyone. Bill and his family could not stay because they did not get their invitation in time to make travel adjustments. They returned to Nashville hoping to make the next Wilkes Reunion.

The Wilkes granddaughters, from left to right, are Nita, Beverly, Pam, Cheryl, Tam, Kim, Rebekka and Shasta.

Craig' sister, Kathy Dale Forrest, has a karioke system which she operated as various family members make requests for songs that they wanted to try to sing. The Wilkes sister sang "You Are My Sunshine." Next year we might sing "The Old Gray Mare, She Ain't What She Used to Be." It turned out that we had some really good performers. Al Branch sang a number of Elvis songs with some Elvis' gestures. The Wilkes grandchildren are making plans for another Wilkes Reunion this year.

We have enjoyed having Conner and David spend two or three days with us due to their having two days off from school because they had met academic expectations while teachers worked with other students. They helped us with several projects in the yard. Today, they will accompany Dee Dee to his McDonald's coffee club. They will play in the play area while Dee Dee visits with his buddies. I will attend my coffee group at Must Be Heaven.

Journal May, 2013

The month of May has been a very good time for us. We enjoyed preparing and anticipating our Sunday School Class (Cornerstone) social at our home. On May 2, we had 30 members come for a covered dish social where much laughing and storytelling took place throughout the house and garage. The Cornerstone class is made up of retirees (anyone our ages would most likely be retired) who are highly educated, strong in their faith, and with many having lived all over the world working as engineers, attorneys, doctors, or serving in the military. They have had a wealth of experience in working and living in many different countries and cultures throughout the U.S. and world.

Our SS teacher is the retired Dean of the TAMU Medical College from Hattiesburg, Miss. He is a Bible scholar graduating William Carey College in Hattiesburg, Miss., a historian who knows the history and the geography of the world. He reads the Bible, Bible commentaries and other writings to prepare to teach the scriptures. Our class members share their insights into the scriptures which lead to some meaningful discussions.

We helped to celebrate long distance three birthdays in our family. On Nita's birthday May 3, Derry and I sang "Happy Birthday" to her. It was very thrilling for her to hear her daddy sing. My sister Dorothy's birthday was May 5, and our granddaughter-in-law Kellye Johnson's birthday was May 21.

May 8 was a big day for Derry and me as we drove over to the Virtual Bookworm Publishing office a couple of miles from our house to receive our first copy of our book, *A Veterinarian's Life and A Veterinarian's Wife*. The book tells our personal stories and includes our genealogies and family trees. We spent approximately six years researching our genealogies and writing our stories. We were so blessed to have had it completed and almost ready for publication before Derry's stroke.

We had the privilege of being invited to the TAMU Nursing School Graduation by one of Derry's caregivers, Curtis Schroller. His family invited us to join the family of 15 for lunch at Madden's in Bryan after the graduation. We got to know his grandparents, parents, aunts, uncles and classmates.

Our biggest celebration during this month was having our dear dear friends, Bill and Velta Morris from Lancaster, SC (originally from Kentwood, La.) who came on Sunday afternoon, May 19, and were with us until Thursday morning. We had four wonderful days of eating, visiting, resting and watching the SEC baseball games. There was really nothing to do but enjoy each other. On Monday, we drove up to The Edge General Store in Edge, TX (about 30 miles east of Bryan/College Station) for a hamburger to see where Velta's brother Claude Gray comes to sing during some nights of entertainment. Claude drives down from Henderson to perform free for benefits to help the family with tremendous hospital bills due to their son being treated for cancer.

As I was driving us back to CS, an 18 wheeler passed us and threw a rock that hit the front passenger's side window where Derry was sitting. The window shattered into a zillion pieces with most of the glass falling outside the SUV. I stopped as soon as I could. Bill very bravely got out on the left side of the SUV into the ongoing traffic to come around to the right side to place a TAMU picnic throw over the window. Velta held it in the back until we came to a place where we could get out and do a better job of covering the window. It made a *pop-pop-pop* sound until we arrived home. The glass company came the next day to our home and replaced the window.

We ended May with a trip to TAMU to attend the A&M Retirees meeting. We joined several hundred who attended the CVM faculty, staff, employees, and students for a barbeque catered by J Cody's. While visiting the Department Head's office, I made pictures of Derry presenting a copy of his book to Dr. Roussel and Gayle Snook and made several pictures of him with veterinary colleagues who were in attendance.

Journal June, 2013

Derry and I began this month helping our neighbors prepare to leave for their two-week vacation in Orlando, Florida. Derry and I wanted to help the mother and the children weed the garden and area next to our fence. The three children and I were busy weeding the garden while Derry and the mother were clearing out some small tree limbs. She noticed and excitedly waved for me to see Derry using his left hand. He told me later that he is now beginning to use the left hand more which is our fervent prayer.

On Monday, the women of the Cornerstone Class met for lunch at Abuelo's Restaurant. The ladies enjoyed the Christian fellowship and food. Conner and David spent the day with us due to having comp days from school.

During an enjoyable conversation with Derry's niece, Dr. Robin Fabre of Tyler, she shared with us that she and Shad had put their house on the market. They are the proud owners of two 50 # boxers and a black and white Fancy Rat whose name is King Charles, a leftover from Lauren's science project. The commitment made by Lauren in this research project was that King Charles would live out his natural life. So the dilemma for them is "What do we do with the dogs and the rat when the realtor shows the house?" Well, each time the realtor calls to show the house, they load the boxers and King Charles into their vehicle and ride around Tyler the air-conditioned vehicle for an hour or until the realtor leaves. The dogs do not like having King Charles riding in the vehicle with them, but they have no choice. What we as parents do for our children!

We are excited to have our first caregiver, Lee McNew, back with us. She had to be off for three months caring for her husband who was recovering from a broken back. Wayne is doing very well and is able to do almost anything that he wants to do with caution. After Derry steps out of the shower, Lee dries and creams his body, helps him get dressed and drives him each morning to the Wellness Center for his routine of therapy and exercise. This gives me time to take care of some food preparation, business, doctor appointments, and print his daily schedule of activities.

Yesterday, Lee mixed up a pan of pork/beans for me to bake this morning for us to take to the JOY luncheon at our church. We added to our food contribution was potato salad from SAM's and cantaloupe. Lee and Derry carried the food in the church while I parked the car. She helped Derry serve his plate and cut his meat. This enabled me to be able to serve my plate and enjoy my lunch with them.

Friday, Derry and I drove to St. Joseph Hospital for Derry's routine appointment with Dr. Schwartz, his cardiologist. Derry's blood pressure was perfect, his heart was in rhythm, his glucose level was good, and his weight remains stable at 210. Dr. Schwartz was so elated to see him in such excellent condition. Dr. Schwartz stated, "You should be the "poster child" for St. Joseph Hospital with your picture on a huge billboard. " Dr. Schwartz gave praise to all of Derry's doctors, to Derry for his determination to recover, and to me for taking such good care of him. As I tell everyone, "Taking care of Derry is a full-time responsibility but one that I enjoy. I would not want to be doing anything else."

Robin and Lauren spent three nights with us while Lauren was preparing to compete in the 4-H Veterinary Science competition at TAMU on Thursday. They were kind enough to stay over Thursday night to help us load the SUV for our Louisiana journey on Friday to spend two nights with sister Elaine. We enjoyed a catfish dinner at Tam and Luke's camp on the Bogue Chitto River Saturday evening. I drove the 525 miles to Washington Parish. This was the first time that I had driven this distance since our medical rehabilitation. Derry and I made the trip just fine without having to make numerous stops along the way. Several months ago, I asked Derry where he would like to travel. He always replied," I want to go to Nashville, TN to see our great-grandchildren. He enjoys visiting Bill and Kellye and her parents, but his greatest desire was for the children to get to know him and for him to get to get to know them and enjoy them.

On Monday, June 17, Bobbie, Elaine, Jan, Derry and I left Mt. Pisgah at 8:00 A.M. with all wearing matching TAMU t-shirts to drive to Nashville, TN. The Aggie t-shirts created some responses from travelers. One man asked if we had Johnny Manziel with us.

Jan did most of the driving because she is accustomed to driving a SUV. We arrived at grandson Bill's home in Lebanon, TN around 6:00 p.m. where Derry and I remained until we returned to Louisiana. Jan, Elaine, and Bobbie checked in at the Wyndham Resort in Nashville. Tuesday morning, Jan and Elaine drove Bobbie to her granddaughter's house in Cookeville where she remained until we left for Louisiana on Sunday morning. We spent six glorious days with our great-grandchildren, Mia and Chase. Derry walked around the block with Kellye, Bill, and Mia, and Chase riding their bicycles. We enjoyed watching them do their thing at the subdivision pool.

Friday night, Kellye's parents, Joani and Dan Staudt, had us over for a steak dinner which we thoroughly enjoyed. Jan and Elaine were so exhausted from some challenging experiences in getting to their hotel that Mr. Staudt hand delivered their steaks to them at the hotel.

Saturday, Jan, Elaine, and I drove to the historic square in downtown Franklin, TN where we visited art galleries, gift shops and had lunch at Meribee's. This was the first time that I had gone out to eat with family without Derry since January 2012. Derry remained home with Kellye, Mia, and Chase. Even though a little apprehensive, Kellye did a super job of seeing that Derry's needs were met.

After an overnight stay in Louisiana, Derry and I returned to College Station on Monday. I was amused at him as he became very talkative as he saw the beauty in everything that we passed. The adjective began with "Isn't that pretty?"to "Isn't that beautiful?" the closer we got to College Station. It was nice being back in Sunday School and church on Sunday. It was also a pleasure seeing our neighbors who had helped water our small garden.

Journal July, 2013

July began a week of putting everything back in place such as medicines, toiletries, clothes, foods after we returned from our La. and Tennessee trip. It works best for two old people to have things where they can find them. Derry is a very routine person, and it is best if we do not change things on him. Each day, Lee, his caregiver, takes him to the Wellness Center for him to do this weight bearing and therapy exercises for his left arm and hand. Lee is a member at the Wellness Center and does her exercises while there. He does the exercises in the same location where he received his OT months ago. The therapists keep an eye on him while he is exercising even though he does not receive the OT.

I found that the machines seem to agitate my back and legs; therefore, I walk in the mall, Lowe's, Sam's, or Walmart. Derry and I went to the mall Monday evening. He walked to the food court with me to get a "no sugar added" Breyer's ice cream. After we ate the ice cream, we walked back to the "bouncing trampoline" for him to watch the children bounce while I made a long fast walking trip around the mall.

July 4 was a nice celebration for us with Patrick's family coming by after lunch for watermelon. Patrick changed out the batteries in our smoke alarms so that the beeping would not keep us awake. He also replaced a spotlight in our den ceiling. Even though he is tall, he still has to use a ladder for the ceiling jobs. We appreciate his help.

After they left our house, they went to the George Bush Library festivities which included: concessions, games, live entertainment, hot air balloon glow, and a magnificent symphony performance followed by the traditional fireworks display.

Derry and I listened to the symphony on the computer playing several of the great patriotic songs and saw the fireworks on screen. We could hear the fireworks from our front porch. Our neighbor's children invited us out to see them shoot some fun sparkles in the driveway, buy we were already dressed for bed. The neighbors drove to George Bush Library to see the fireworks.

We had flags flying all around our house from the flag pole that Ross restored, four flags in our flower urns in front, one from the stand on the front of our house, and the one mounted in the yard by the Lions Club.

July 5 was Derry's day as he reached 79 years of age. Sandra Wynn brought him the traditional sugar free apple pie that she prepares for him each year. We drove to Navasota to look for a recliner for Dora and ate at a Mexican restaurant (not the best) before returning home.

July 6, I drove us (Derry, Bruce and Diane Miles, and me) to Huntsville to a furniture store where I found a Flex Steel recliner that I think will do. I will wait until Sept 5 to order it because the factory puts on a national 40% sale. We ate at a seafood restaurant in Huntsville before returning home. Derry had two days of eating out in celebration of his birthday.

On July 17, Derry had visits with Dr. Hosea, podiatrist and Dr. Niemann, neurologist. Dr. Ramirez, his first neurologist, left CS to become a neuro-hospitalist in another city. We established a relationship with Dr. Niemann, his new neuro doctor, and learned more about how the brain recovers, etc. He examined Derry and found that he has sensory in all parts of his body and stated that the affected arm and hand are usually the last parts to recover. No one knows why the brain recovers the way that it does, but we are very grateful that Derry's body is recovering.

July 20 was a very challenging morning for us. We were on our way to the Wellness Center when I did not pay closer attention to the message center in the SUV. It told me that the Liftglass or the Liftdoor was not closed. I just assumed that we had accidentally hit the Liftglass button on the vehicle entry control. I stated that I would close the Liftglass when we got to the restaurant. I backed out with the Liftglass up and bent the garage door beyond repair. We continued with our trip to eat after Derry managed to get the garage door raised high enough so that we could back out. The garage door remained open until the American Door came Monday and installed a new insulated door with a new motor for opening and closing the garage door. We are enjoying the quiet sound as the new door is opened and closed. We have become *overly* conscious of making sure the liftglass is closed before backing out. We were very blessed that the lifegate was not damaged. The paint in that area had some tiny scratches. The new insulated door seems to keep the garage cooler.

July 26, Dr. Mitchell performed a vein ablation procedure on my (Dora) varicose vein on my left leg. I had the right ablation done a year ago. The procedure went well and so has my recovery. Our caregiver Lee McNew drove us to and from the procedure. After we returned home, Lee told us that fire had destroyed their home the afternoon before. She did not call us to tell us what had happened because she knew we would insist that she not come and that we would have insisted that they come to spend the night at our house. The insurance company provided a hotel for them. Lee and her husband Wayne are sorting through the rubbish to see what can be used.

LaBridget and her aunt Sheila came and picked up the two single beds with pads and sheets to be used for her grandchildren. Now that we have the beds removed from that bedroom, we plan to have men come and move the couch from the den upstairs into that bedroom which will become a TV and sitting room for guests and a place for Derry and me to watch movies.

Best Buy will deliver our new 55" flat screen TV for our den. Hopefully, we will be able to see Johnny Manziel perform and during basketball season we will be able to watch Lebron James with the Miami Heat perform.

Journal August, 2013

August has been one of the hottest months ever—it seems. We received an analysis from the city of College Station showing that we have used too much water in the yard. We called Jennifer Nations, the consultant, and invited her out to see why we are using so much water. She found that some of the sprinkler heads needed gaskets, some were too low in the grass causing the water to just run under the grass and out into the street, and some heads were damaged from possibly the lawn mowers.

The house is approximately 18 years old which means that it was time for a sprinkler system overhaul. Dan Beltrand, our yard maintenance supervisor, came and replaced several of the sprinkler heads. He also installed a new sprinkler system controller which will help. Hopefully, we will have a reduced water bill for the yard. We watered six tomato plants and two cucumber vines that did not bear the first vegetable. No more vegetable garden! That is where much of the water cost came from.

Lee continues accompanying Derry to the Wellness Center each morning for his therapy and exercises while I maintain things at home. Jennifer Schilling and the children came by for a visit. We gave Kathryn her birthday card to help her celebrate her August 8 birthday. We attended the Cornerstone Class ice cream party at the church on Friday evening.

Suddenlink technician came by and installed the HD box for our new TV. We are thoroughly enjoying the large 55"screen, seeing so many details that happen on the football field, golf course, cooking shows, etc. We can actually watch a player make a touchdown without having to wait for the referee's signal.

We delivered Jim Dixon's homemade cookies for his 80th birthday and cookies to Ms. Virgie Perryman (95 years old) who is recovering from cataract surgery. I visited our dentist and learned that I have an abcess around one of my tooth implants. He prescribed a special mouth wash that I am using three or four times a day before my appointment with the periodontist on Monday.

Today, August 19, I saw Dr. Wiley, periodontist, and learned that I have an infection in the area around the implant but the x-ray showed that the implant is very secure in the bone and is not a problem. When I go back, he will make an incision in the gum, remove the infected tissue, scrape the bone, possibly do some bone graft, and treat it with a special medicine and antibiotics. He assured me that I would be fine once he removed the infected tissue. From the x-ray he noticed that I have large sinuses which did not cause the infection. My osteoporosis did not cause the infection. He commented that I do a good job of keeping my implant area very clean. The reason for the infection was caused by my eating a cracker without my bottom plate one night. A cracker crumb got between the implant and the gum causing the infection. This was an expensive lesson for me to learn.

Today, I called Animal Control to report that we have had a wild pig (6 months old) in our backyard eating sunflower seeds that Derry broadcast over the ground under the bird feeders for the cardinals and blue jays because they can't feed from the squirrel-proof bird feeders. Officer Gentry from Animal Control came out and assessed our situation. He emphasized that there is not anything that the city can legally do. The city and the citizens cannot shoot a gun in the city. When they find a deer hung on the top of an iron fence, they have to use a knife to kill it to remove it. He stated that we could buy a trap for a few hundred dollars and try to trap him, but we would have to arrange for someone to come and get the pig from the trap. He reported that they have run some out of the Walmart parking lot near us and several from the TAMU campus. After realizing that we were baiting the wild varmints, we do not discard any scraps or sow any feed on the ground. We have *stopped!* The officer recommended a bull horn to scare the animals away.

Today I went for my yearly mammogram which was not as painful and uncomfortable as in the past. On August 22, I will visit with my joint and pain doctor briefly to write a referral for me to see how my back is dong after a year of Forteo injections. I will go Sept. 11 for the bone density test.

On Sunday, August 25, we took a huge birthday cake out to Pat and Jennifer's in remembrance of the entire family's birthdays beginning July 4 and ending Sept. 3. They took the cake to their church fellowship.

Grandson Ross flew to Chicago with his Ava Maria football team where they played the Robert Morris University. Nita flew up and was there for Ross since Steve was involved coaching his team in Miami. Grandson Bill and his family and in-laws just returned from several days of vacation at the Wyndham at Panama City, Florida. His children want to move there where they could enjoy the beach and other activities every day.

Journal September, 2013

Monday, Sept. 2 Derry treated me to lunch at Olive Garden for my September 1 birthday. We did not want to fight the football crowd on Sunday for my birthday lunch. The Wellness Center was closed for Labor Day so we got in a little walk. Tuesday, Odessa, our incredible care giver from Comfort Keepers came and completed several household chores while I took Derry to exercise. We attended our coffee clubs at 2:30 P.M.

Wednesday was our big day! After exercise, we drove about forty miles out in the country to eat the best barbeque ever at the Blue Moon café. Blue Moon is about ten miles from The Edge General Store in the other direction. Derry stated, "Dora, we would have never stopped at the Blue Moon if we had been riding around looking for an eating place." Once we entered the small eating area, we were greeted by the friendly owner with whom we placed our order. They cook collards fresh on

Wednesday which were delicious. The potato salad was homemade, and the ribs were out of this world. They have two or three tables (from someone's kitchen or dining room with a variety of unmatched chairs) in this small eating room which provides the opportunity to get to know others who are eating there. Blue Moon has a tremendous take-out business. An oil drilling employee came for several box lunches that were packaged in a large cardboard box as take-outs. They say "If you prepare good food, the people will come." This is certainly true of Blue Moon.

We also attended an update meeting by a RCI rep at Johnny Carino's restaurant with a free dinner which was a great disappointment to the salesman when we refused to transfer our Silverleaf Resorts deeded property in exchange for points.

After that long day, I asked Derry what he wanted to do on Thursday. His reply, "I want to stay at home." Thursday—after exercise, "stay at home" is exactly what we did. We spent a quiet enjoyable day doing the usual chores around the house. Friday— After exercise, we grocery shopped for items that we needed for preparing food for two families who have serious illnesses in their families. I made a lime pie and a lemon pie, homemade potato salad and baked beans to go with the sliced ham. Derry and I delivered the meals Saturday afternoon.

We received a call Saturday afternoon from grandson Ross who was calling to wish me a belated birthday. He and Nita were driving to Naples for supper after Ross and his team had completed their football game at Ava Maria. Nita drove over from Miami alone to watch Ross play because Jennifer was working and Steve's team was playing a game. It was nice hearing from him and getting a report on his first week of classes.

Ave Maria football team played on the high school field near the Ave Maria University. Ross made some plays which he and Nita enjoyed. This next week Nita and Steve will drive over for his game. After the game, he will make an overnight trip home and return for football recap on Sunday afternoon.

Sept. 11, I went to St. Joseph's for a bone density test—don't have results yet. Sept. 12, I was treated to lunch at Pei Wei by a good friend Zanna Bickham—one of the few times I have had lunch outside the home with a friend. Sept. 13, we took Derry's left ear hearing aid to be repaired. Dr. Herring found that it did not need to be repaired—the battery case was loose in the hearing aid. Derry is now cruising with two hearing aids.

The Schilling family came on Saturday and watched the TAMU/Alabama game on our HD large screen. We were so pleased with Johnny Manziel's performance and congratulated Alabama on the win. We just have to improve defensively if we want to win the National Championship (Ha!).

Lee took Derry for his visit with Dr. Hosea, Podiatrist on Sept. 19 and will take him to his exercises on the four days that she is here. I take him on Tuesday each week. Dr. Wiley discharged me after making sure the dental implant incision had completely healed. Wednesday, I accompanied my neighbor Salma to FBC where the Discovery Program of Brazos Valley is held for international wives to help them learn about the American culture. Over twenty classes are taught by volunteers who teach sewing, quilting, crocheting, knitting, conversational English, English as a Second Language, etc. Salma registered to attend an English class and a sewing class. Salma was a medical doctor in Syria before moving to the U.S. with her husband Dr. Khaled who is a Neonatologist at Scott and White. They are very good neighbors to us.

Thursday, Derry and I attended the TAMU Retirees Club held at Rudder Tower. Architects from TAMU presented a program, "Heritage as the Key to the Future: Architecture at Texas A&M University." They discussed the underlying design principles of the 2004 Plan and its evolution over its ten-year life, and described the current operational process that guides decisions on the future of the physical form of campus. They explained how the application of the Campus Master Plan and its design guidelines shape the design of new buildings and the restoration of older structures. Their focus in the presentation was to show the challenges in rehabilitating the 1931 Williams Building, so that it can assume its earlier role as the central administration building for the university. As they began reconstruction of this landmark, they discovered beautiful ceilings and stained glass windows that had been covered by some modern remodeling. Derry and I plan to visit these reconstructed buildings on campus as they are completed.

We are feverishly making plans to travel to Franklinton, La. on October 12 where we will stay with my sister Elaine Cook during the week of the Franklinton Fair and Wilkes Family Reunion. Nita will fly to New Orleans from Miami, FL where we will meet her on Sunday. She is very excited to be able to spend a week visiting with her daddy and other family and friends in the area. She will fly back to Miami on October 21. We will return to CS on October 22.

My household project last week was hemming the selvages of the towels in our bath area. The towels are six years old and are washed quite frequently. The towels are perfectly good except for the sides raveling a bit. Lee, our caregiver, brought her good old Singer sewing machine that has steel parts for me to use. It will sew over any challenging fabrics which have allowed me to complete the project. My little Singer made in China does not get the job done. Thank you Lee!

Ross and his Ave Maria football team played Warner University, FL in Lake Wales, Florida on Saturday and won. Ross made some good plays as defensive end. He wears his dad's football number 83 that his dad Steve wore playing defensive end for Mississippi College, Clinton, MS in the 1970's. Nita and Steve drove up for the game and drove Ross back to Ave Maria after the game. It made a nice drive for the family. Ross' team will play Concordia College at Selma, AL next Saturday.

We received some good rain during a thunder storm Saturday evening just as TAMU and Arkansas were beginning to play. Due to an electrical outage throughout our area, we missed part of the game. The electrical outage time was mainly during halftime; therefore, we did not miss many plays. It's time to prepare for our trip to La.

Journal November 11-31, 2013

October was a busy month and an enjoyable one for us. We celebrated 61 years of marriage on October 11. After completing all doctor visits and assessing medication supply and with Lee's help, we began organizing and packing clothing for ten days in

Louisiana. We left College Station on Saturday, October 12 and arrived at Elaine Cook's home around 5:00 p.m.

On Sunday, we drove to New Orleans to meet Nita at the airport for a 12:00 noon arrival from Miami, FL. Sister Elaine accompanied us. After picking up Nita, we drove to the Café de Monde in Jackson Square for coffee and beignets which is something that Nita looks forward to. Her husband Steve reminded us that if Nita gets within 150 miles of the Café de Monde, he has to take her. I questioned him why he always did that. His response, "I like to go there also."

When Nita was a young girl whose orthodontist practiced in a building just off Canal Boulevard in New Orleans, we did several tours around the French Quarter area (wax museum, art shops, clothing stores, and of course, Jackson Square). We saw "Mary Poppins" in the Seanger Theatre. She has some fond memories of visiting N.O.

Derry was born in N.O. and lived there until he was twelve. He detests going back to the city, but for his daughter, he was willing to walk several blocks from the parking lot to get to stand in a long line for coffee and beignets. We survived the trip to and from N.O. Middendorf's Seafood Restaurant at Manchac was not open on Sunday so we stopped at a good Mexican restaurant in Amite, La. We finally made it back to Elaine's for Nita to get unpacked and all of us to get a good night's sleep.

Nita drove Derry to Kentwood to visit with Dr. Keller and to visit the Line Creek Cemetery where Derry's parents are buried and where we will be buried. After they left Kentwood, they drove to a nursery out from Amite, La. that sister Bobbie recommended.

Nita and I rummaged through Dirt Cheap for an hour before we did some grocery shopping while Derry and Elaine remained at her house. It was so much fun! I just wished our granddaughter Jennifer had been with us. Jennifer and I love to "root" together. When we go to Miami next year during the fall season, she and I will do some "rooting."

Tuesday afternoon, Derry and I met some dear friends from Poplarville, Miss. We had not seen them since the 1970's. Sonny and Juanita Knight lived in Kentwood for a few years which gave

65

us some good times together, such as attending the LSU football games and eating and visiting in their home. Juanita is a really good cook and loves to prepare food and watch Derry eat everything that she has cooked. She always thought that it was her cooking that he enjoyed so much, but she learned later that he just enjoys eating and a lot of it anywhere. We laughed together as we recalled things that we had experienced together. They put on their bucket list a trip to CS in the near future.

Wednesday was the day our family brought food to my sister Jan's art studio behind her home which is on the corner across from the Washington Parish Fairgrounds. We visited with sisters, their children, their grandchildren, and even some great-grandchildren. Several cousins, dear friends, and Aunt Margaret Burch came by for a visit.

Saturday was the designated day for our official Earl and Willie Wilkes family reunion at Jan's. After eating hamburgers grilled by Craig Forrest, the parents of younger children walked over to the Fair where they enjoyed the rides, Old McDonald's Farm, etc. The slow-moving adults remained in comfortable chairs at Jan's. We could hear from Jan's all of the music and stage performances from her yard. I was so thrilled to see and visit with nephew Christopher Wilkes, wife Heather, and daughters from Hattiesburg. Chris' interviews with my parents many years ago, provided me very detailed and personal experiences of my parents which we included in our book, "A Veterinarian's Life and A Veterinarian's Wife." When I returned home, I copied several genealogical documents and mailed to him. It appears that he will be the generational keeper of the Wilkes records in the future. I encouraged him and his family to come to CS to see what he would like to copy for his files.

Nita stayed for the night stage performers each evening while Derry, Elaine, and I returned to Elaine's in the late afternoon. Nita thoroughly enjoyed every minute of the fair. She made many pictures with her iPad to take back to show her family. She visited with all of her cousins and their families. Robin, Derry's niece, drove up from Covington, La. and enjoyed the Fair with Nita and other family members. Nita and Robin plan to return to the Fair next year.

On Sunday, we drove to Ponchatoula for a delicious lunch of fried chicken and red beans prepared by Nolan, Jane, and Melody. We enjoyed an extended visit with them. We enjoyed seeing their greenhouse that they had built. We know that Nolan will have an early garden with the greenhouse which will allow him to plant seeds and plants early.

On Monday, we drove Nita to the airport for her return to Miami. Derry, Elaine, and I stopped at Cracker Barrel in Hammond for lunch before returning to Mt. Pisgah.

Tuesday morning, Derry and I began our journey back to CS. After we left Beaumont driving up through the country on 105, I asked Derry if he would like to try his hand at driving. He quickly said, "Yes." When we got to a good place to exchange drivers, we did. He drove a few miles before his right arm and shoulder began to ache. We were not able to adjust the driver's seat to make it comfortable for him. We will have this problem corrected. He continually stated how beautiful everything was: the trees, grass, pastures, and homes. I was relating this experience to a friend when Derry chimed in, "I was so glad to be coming home that everything looked so beautiful to me."

Our caregiver Lee came Wednesday morning and helped us finish unpacking and put everything in its place so that we could continue with our home routine.

Derry and I enjoyed the time with Nita and the rest of the families. We appreciated sister Elaine for putting up with us for ten days. Only a sister would do this. She along with our other siblings Bobbie, Faye, Jan, Chuck, and Derry's sister and family are very special people. We thank God for them!

Journal November 4-25, 2013

We are finally getting back into the swing of things after our ten days in Louisiana. I finally removed all of Derry's clothes that he wore when he weighed 260 lbs. He now weighs 205 and plans to keep his present weight which allows him to sleep without his C-pap. I took his large clothes to the St. Vincent de Paul shop in downtown Bryan. The store sells these items for Catholic charities. I took some of my large clothes to the church to be taken to a mission in the Dakotas.

When Derry went to his dentist for a cleaning, they found that he has a cavity which did not require a root canal. Dr. Williams requested that he come in every three months for the cleaning since he is unable to floss his teeth effectively with one hand.

Malek AC technician came Wednesday morning to evaluate the heating system before we turned on the heat. We are pleased that we have heat since our weather is down in the low 40's tonight

I drove Derry to the church today to attend the FBC's Financial Oversight Committee of which he is a member. After lunch, we settled down in our chairs for an afternoon rest. I enjoyed a nice telephone visit with granddaughter Jennifer who was checking on us. A couple of days ago, we enjoyed a telephone visit from grandson Bill who was checking to see how we were doing.

Steve's team Christopher Columbus won their game this week in Miami and will play a district play-off game next week. Ross's football team Ava Maria University traveled to Georgia beating the opponent. Next week Ross and team will travel to Virginia for a game.

We enjoyed watching the Texas Aggies defeat Mississippi State today. Manziel performed in his amazing way of quarterbacking. This was the last home game for the Aggies this year. The pros are anxiously watching and waiting for Manziel to make the decision to go pro at the end of this year. He is enjoyable to watch. We feel so privileged to have had him play for TAMU. He has brought a great deal of excitement to the game of football and to the fans and community and even around the country.

As of the week of November 4, Derry's left side seems to have made some important progress in his gaining more use in the left hand and in the left side. He seems to swallow better and his speech seems to be stronger. He is naturally using the left hand more without being conscious of doing so. God is continuing to completely heal him in several ways.

He has been preparing some of his meals, making and bringing me coffee to my chair, and is more engaged in seeing things that need to be done. He mixed up spray and sprayed the roses and fertilized them. He filled up the bird feeders by himself. This allowed me to rest for two or three hours. Sunday, he located the gate key to the lake and removed the lock and chain for the workers who will be replacing the fence. Our HOA owns the fence that surrounds the lake and on both sides of Woodcreek Drive. Each resident has had to pay a portion of the cost of the replacement even though their property does not back up to the lake. I have been saddened by this arrangement that stands because it is written into the legal guidelines when the subdivision was formed.

Lee McNew, our caregiver, and I spent Monday morning taking out all china, crystal, and other items from the hutches and putting them back after Lee cleaned the mirrors and glass. Some of the items that are not family keepsakes will find a new home. We now have everything ready for our Friday night dinner (supper) for Lee and her family. There will be ten of us.

Derry had two skin spots on his face biopsied and results are that they are squamous cell carcinomas and will be removed by Dr.Shook on December 17.

Thursday, November 21, 2013

We attended Dr. Green's brunch honoring the retired veterinarians which was held in the Mark Francis Room at the Vet school. Derry especially enjoyed visiting with colleagues with whom he worked for 17 years. It was a fun time for me as well since I have always been a part of his work there in helping to build relationships with the spouses, staff, and the veterinarians. We have had many of them in our home for social events and several have stopped by to visit Derry on occasions. Dr. Roussel reminded us that the Large Animal Dept. would be having the traditional Christmas luncheon on December 20 in the Large Animal Hospital and will be expecting to see us there. I assured him that we would be there.

My nephew Patrick Schilling and his family came to join us for Thanksgiving. It was a wonderful day for all of us. Kathryn is two years old and has captured our hearts. She gets the picture album from the coffee table and crawls up in my lap to look at the family pictures. She soon learned who Mia and Chase are as we went through the album. Connor and David enjoyed throwing the football and shooting baskets in the driveway. The weather was rather cold which kept them coming in periodically to warm up.

We enjoyed the Harvest banquet at our church on November 24. On November 25, we were guests of our neighbors, Dr. and Mrs. Hilal, Noura, Yousef, and Sarah, for a delicious dinner. They were kind to prepare the foods that Derry could eat. We not only enjoyed the dinner but enjoyed visiting with Khalid and Salma and the three children. It had been a while since we heard from the Hilal children about some of their activities. Noura has a part in the "Fiddler on the Roof" that the A&M Consolidated Choir will perform in February. We plan to attend. The Hilals are wonderful friends and neighbors. We are very blessed to have them next door.

Lee has been helping to decorate the house for Christmas. She hung the wreaths on the lanterns on the front of the house and decorated the stairs. She plans to retire on December 20. We will miss her tremendously as one of Derry's caregivers. She and her husband Wayne are our friends and will be checking on us from time to time. Lee loves plants and takes care of the plants in the planters, on the porches, and in the yard. She helps Derry keep the birds fed and watered in addition to all of the things she does for Derry and me in caring for us.

We were saddened to learn that a close friend and former dentist, Dr. Stephen Bryan, passed away last week. Derry and I visited with Steve and Cathy a couple of times in Austin when Derry's was in Austin for the heart ablations about three years ago. We are hoping to get Cathy to come to CS for a visit.

Journal December 2-25, 2013

December 2, I drove Derry to St. Joseph to have his blood drawn in preparation for his visit with his cardiologist, Dr. Schwartz on Friday, Dec. 6. Upon our return from the lab, I fixed pancakes for us before he and Lee left to go to Dr. Hosea's office for his podiatry visit. I remained home taking care of business in the office.

December 6, while visiting with Dr. Schwartz, he reprimanded us for coming in with almost freezing temperature with occasional rain. The lab results identified an increase in Derry's cholesterol which is not good. Dr. Schwartz really fussed at Derry and made us get back on the foods that will not raise his cholesterol. If his cholesterol has not improved by June, 2014, he will be forced to increase his medication which he does not want to do. Derry reassured him that he would get it under control. Dr. Schwartz again praised us both for the tremendous job we have done in restoring Derry to his health.

December 7 "Cutting a donut!" When Derry got ready to take his bedtime meds at 9:00 p.m., he found that he was out of Benadryl which helps him to sleep along with the Ambien, etc. The temperature was 31 degrees. I asked him if he just had to have them. He stated that he must have them to sleep. We put on our overcoats, shawl, and caps and headed across the interstate to Walgreen's. As we were crossing over the bridge, evidently I sped up some to avoid the upcoming traffic light change. All of a sudden, we skidded across into the opposite lane and headed for the side of the bridge. I hit the brakes and the steering wheel turned one way and then another. All of a sudden, the vehicle turned around, facing in the opposite direction and stopped. We had cut a "donut."

Thank God there were no vehicles traveling in either direction. We did not hit the bridge which meant there was no damage to the vehicle. Since, we were headed back to Woodcreek in the direction of our house, I just slowly drove down and turned around and headed back to Walgreen's. Derry reminded me that a bridge ices over because it is not on the ground. We returned home with the Benadryl and reflected on what had just happened. Derry asked me if I had turned the steering wheel, and I told him that I had. He stated, "Someone took control." As we were praying this morning after our Bible readings, we thanked God for His favor and his protection over us. We gave up going out Sunday morning to SS and church since we still had a freezing temperature. *Good Idea!*

This experience reminded me of my brother Chuck as a teenager loved "cutting a donut" on the Mt. Hermon highway. I told Derry that I had to call Chuck and let him know that I had "cut a donut." Our daddy had bought the family a beautiful new white Chrysler. He noticed one day how worn the tires were and learned that Chuck had been "cutting donuts" with the car. I am not sure what the outcome was, but I can imagine that Daddy took care of the "fun."

December 11 began with trips to the Texas Cardiac office in Bryan to see Dr. Horton and his P.A. They retrieved the TEE results from Dr. Schwartz that he had done several months before. The results showed that there is still a small flow but nothing to worry about. They will see him in a year. Lee drove Derry to Bryan for his visit with Dr. Hosea, his podiatrist.

December 12 was a big day preparing for twelve friends for dinner. Lee and I had prepared most of the food on Wednesday. I baked pies Wednesday evening. Wayne, Lee's husband, came to help put in the stakes to support the two large white reindeer in our back yard. They do not have a place to display them, so they brought them to us to display. They are beautiful and can be seen from the other side of the lake.

We enjoyed having Jennifer S. and the children spend the day with us. Jennifer had two doctor appointments. Conner and David came in handy helping Wayne with the ties attaching the extension cords to the steel frames. They also helped Lee plant two white cyclamen plants in the urns in the front. While the children were here, I told them that I wanted them to go through the Christmas boxes in the garage and take anything that they wanted. Kathryn found two containers of pink garland and was adamant about taking them home. It was a real thrill seeing them go through the boxes and finding decorations that they wanted. I warned Jennifer that we were going to do this, but that I would have a large plastic container for them to transport them. The box will allow easy storage after Christmas. Patrick reported that Kathryn had enjoyed playing with the beautiful dolls that can be used on the tree for decorations.

December 12 All 14 members of our "Hamburger Group" came and enjoyed a delicious dinner and great time of Christian fellowship. Several of them called and wrote to us to say how much they had enjoyed the evening. Derry thanked the group for their prayers and support during our recuperation from our medical challenges. They responded by stating that now Derry and I are praying and supporting them in medical issues that their family members are experiencing. "What goes around comes around!"

December 17 Because I was sick with a sore throat and sinus infection, Lee came to our house at 7:30 a.m. to take Derry to Dr. Shook's office to have the two squamous cell carcinomas removed from his temple and nose. The office told us that he would be there two-four hours checking after each removal to make certain they got everything.

It did take four hours. After each cancer removal, they froze the tissue and determined the next move. They had to remove the cancer on his right temple three times before they had it all removed. Derry had 13 stitches in his temple and seven on his nose. Odessa, another caregiver, arrived at 9:00 a.m. and served Derry's meal. She changed bedding, did laundry, and vacumned.

Comfort Keepers delivered us a beautiful array of boxes filled with goodies. We will share these boxes with our caregivers, since Derry is diabetic and has to eat his special goodies. Lee's last day with us was Friday, December 20. We will miss her, but she will be around when needed. Lee and I made several pounds of candy for her to have during the holidays and to share with friends. We made Martha Washington candy filled with coconut or pecans. Thursday night, I made her a large recipe of Chocolate Chip Cookies, and she made "snickerdoodles" which were very good.

December 21 Pat and Jennifer brought the children by at 12:00 noon while they did some Christmas shopping. Connor and David were able to visit Yousef and his family next door for a few minutes. Kathryn is incredibly smart and a joy to keep. She keeps all of us in line.

December 22, Due to the time that it takes to re-bandage Derry's incision, we decided that we just did not have the strength and stamina to get ready and make the 8:30 a.m. service. So, we stayed at home and watched four church services and heard some great preaching and singing. Hopefully, by next Sunday we will be back in the swing of things.

I made pecan pies and cookies for the Hilals and Schillings. After I return from taking Derry to have stitches removed Monday afternoon, I will make more to share with Dr. and Mrs. Boysen, our neighbors. This should finish most of the cooking to be done during this Christmas season.

During Thanksgiving week, we were listening to one of the ministers on TV. He told an interesting story that all parents whose children live a great distant from their home could relate to. Derry and I had a great laugh!

It goes like this! A father called his son who was living in a faraway state and told him that he was divorcing his mother. He stated that they had been married over 30 years, and he could not go on any longer. The son called his sister who was in another state and told her what their father was doing. The daughter called her father and told him not to do anything before she and her brother could get there for Thanksgiving. The father looked at his wife and stated, "They are coming for Thanksgiving, and we do not have to pay their way."

December 23 Derry and I ate at Fish Daddy's and wished each other "Merry Christmas!" On *December 24* we plan to have an early dinner at Olive Garden and then attend the Candlelight Service at our church at 6:00 p.m. We will again wish each other a "Merry Christmas!"

Our dear friend Velta Morris is faithful to forward pictures of our great-grandchildren that are posted on Facebook. She sent one of Chase sitting on the kitchen cabinet with his feet in Kellye's sink of dishwater. Kellye had turned her back for about five minutes and discovered Chase enjoying a "footwashing" in the sink. Derry stated, "Chase is now ready to be a "footwashing" Baptist. We really enjoyed the picture.

Christmas Day we received calls from the Steve Johnson family who are enjoying Christmas in Nashville with Bill, Kellye, Mia, and Chase. Derry and I were so pleased that they could all be together. Steve, Nita, Jennifer, and Ross will begin the long journey back to Miami on Friday. Derry and I enjoyed the quietness and convenience of our home on Christmas Day! When one has experienced many medical challenges, home is the place to be.

Kelly Boysen, our neighbor's daughter, came over on Christmas Eve afternoon with some delicious goodies that her mother had made. We enjoyed her visit and got caught up on all of the things going on in her life as she anticipates graduating A&M in May. We are very proud of her and for her. She is such a pleasant and sweet young lady. She was an elementary student at SWV Elementary School where I served.

We took cookies, pecan pie, and a Cajun roasted turkey breast to Sandra and Gerald as they were preparing for their family members to arrive. They have a total of nine when they all gather. Her living area is beautifully decorated with the normal decorations with a cabbage doll dressed in Christmas clothes and two antique German dolls given to her by Corrie Bruce. The dolls were dressed in antique crocheted sweaters and caps standing under the grouping of three Christmas trees. We were so pleased that the Wynn family came by after having their pictures made so that we could see them all dressed in their outfits designed especially for the family picture. Derry kept stating that he was so pleased that the family came by.

We are looking forward to having Patrick and his family and our neighbors, the Hilals, for New Year's Day luncheon. Connor and David enjoy playing and visiting with the Hilal children, Noura, Sarah, and Yousef. The family enjoys Kathryn when she visits us from time to time. We don't have many small children around us.

Derry and I praise God for all of the answered prayers for us, for those around us in College Station, our family in Miami, FL, our family in Nashville, TN, our family members in Louisiana, and our good friends in other states. We wish all of you continued good health, happiness, contentment, and God's blessings throughout the year.

Journal January, 2014

The most exciting event for us and many football fans was the New Year's Eve football game between Texas A&M and Duke in the Chick-Fil-A Bowl. We were so disappointed at A&M's performance at the end of the first half. Our son-in-law Steve called us from Miami and stated that they had announced on the news that the A&M Defense bus was broken down and had not arrived.

It looked as though we did not have a defense on the field. But, something happened in the Aggie dressing room during the halftime. The second half was a different story based on players motivating each other to never quit. They didn't quit and the defense did show up, in fact, a defensive player intercepted the ball from Duke which ultimately won the game for A&M. I was congratulating my sisters in Louisiana on the Saints win when they interrupted me by saying that the most exciting game for them was the Johnny Manziel's performance and TAMU's win.

New Year's Day was a pleasure for us as we were joined for lunch by Patrick's family and the Hilal family next door. We enjoyed turkey, Texas caviar, mashed potatoes, green mixed salad, Salma's homemade humas, plus several pies for dessert. It was a good time for the children and adults to be together.

Due to the cold weather, we remained home during Sunday morning where we enjoyed several worship services on TV. Friday, we enjoyed working with Derry's new caregiver who helped with many chores around the house.

Monday, January 5, I was able to leave the house for two hours running errands and came back to a very clean and orderly house.

Wednesday, January 7 Derry accompanied me for my check-up with Dr. Richard Smith. Dr. Smith checked my records and reported that I do have osteoarthritis and that my recent bone density test revealed that my bone density had improved 25% since my last test. He stated that within seven months I will be at the end of the two years allowed for Forteo injections and will receive another bone density. I will see him on September 17 to learn if my bones have improved. He stated that if the bone density shows 50% improvement, it will be a wonderful report.

It was exciting to receive a basketball game schedule from Mia. Her mother and daddy are her coaches for the Panthers (a church team). Their eighth game will be their last game on March 1, 2014. I was so surprised to see one of the teams named Kangaroos. We were the Kentwood Kangaroos at Kentwood High. We also received a basketball schedule for Connor and

David in Caldwell. We plan to drive over to see them play if the weather allows. It sounds as though the Wilkes basketball tradition continues through the great-grandchildren.

Derry gets up around 5:00 a.m. or 6:00 a.m. and take his blood pressure and glucose by himself. This allows me more hours of sleep before getting up. If I get up before he takes his vital signs, I do them for him.

As Mary, our caregiver, sat down in a chair by the bedroom window to put on Derry's support socks, she noticed a hawk flying and perched on the fence. The hawk flew up in a large tree next door. Mary showed Derry and me where the hawk was. All of a sudden the hawk flew down into our yard swooping up a small bird that was feeding in our yard. The wrens and other birds come in flocks to the bird feeders that Derry keeps filled for them. It provides a great opportunity for the prey to get a meal. Derry plans to move one of the feeders farther under the bushes to provide more protection for the birds.

We went upstairs to our sitting room/den and watched again Secretariat, a Walt Disney DVD. We enjoyed being upstairs and felt as though we had been to a movie theatre. I placed several of our videos in the small drawers of the chest that holds the TV. We have a VCR downstairs with our large TV, but we just wanted to watch the movie upstairs. Derry especially likes it when I am not jumping up and down doing things. Upstairs created a place of quietness and calmness with no interruptions.

This morning, we drove to Physician Centre to have Dee Dee's blood drawn in preparation for a visit with Dr. James Bonds on Wednesday. This afternoon, Derry was evaluated by his OT Carol who was very excited to have him again as her client. She was truly amazed at how much he is using his left hand. He will be seeing Carol for therapy on M-W-F for six weeks. Carol commented, "Your brain is healing." She noticed that he is much more aware of things around him rather than focusing on himself. I shared with Carol on how he is conscious of helping me with laundry, fixing my coffee, and filling my water mug.

During our visit with Dr. Bonds, he stopped Derry's diabetes medicine based on the results of Derry's fasting bloodwork. We are checking his glucose level twice a day just to make sure it remains in the proper range. Dr. Bonds stated, "Due to your walking, exercise, and diet, you have eliminated the need for diabetes medicine." *Hallelujah!* This week was also Derry's visit to Dr. Hosea, Podiatrist and my dental visit for teeth cleaning.

We called Mia and Chase and sang "Happy Birthday" to each of them. They had their separate family parties on their birthdays (December 10 and January 17), but they had a joint friends balloon party Saturday at their subdivision club house.

Monday, January 20 Derry attended OT with Carol. Thursday, he had an eye check-up with Dr. Perkins who stated that his exam was perfect. He has not lost any more vision due to diabetes. *Praise God!*

Friday, January 24 Thirteen ninth and tenth graders and two leaders who were participating in Disciple-Now arrived at our house with their blankets, sleeping bags and pillows. After they visited the five rooms with beds, they chose where they would like to sleep and put down their beddings..

January 31, we will travel to Hammond, La. to spend the night. We will be very close to Ponchatoula where we will visit Jane and Nolan. Saturday, we will drive to Kentwood to attend the 50th Wedding Anniversary of Dr. and Mrs. Carl Keller. Dr. Keller and Derry were veterinary and business partners for over forty years. We will travel back to College Station on Sunday, February 2.

Journal March, 2014

Derry completed his allowed OT sessions on March 9 which makes him happy. He was so tired of pulling small beads out of a piece of silly putty with his left thumb and index finger. His OT knew that I was massaging his left hand and fingers daily on our side porch in the double swing and remarked that I was truly his OT. He is resolved to consciously use the left hand more which will strengthen the arm and hand. He is amazingly unloading the dishwasher, doing some laundry, and helping me with planting flowers in the outside urns. I take him daily to the Wellness Center to complete his cardio exercises.

Derry went through the slides that he had accumulated while on the faculty at TAMU and those from Kentwood Veterinary Clinic. He selected the slides that he chose to keep to possibly use in more writings. We discarded the slides that he did not want to keep. It is a good feeling to successfully go through files and records that we have kept and can now discard. We have some other items that we want go through as we have time. I told Derry that I do not want Nita left with having to go through things that would not mean anything to her. We kept what we feel is important to family.

Derry's nephew Jody Fabre has sent us several pictures of his daughter Colleen riding her horse. She is quite the horse (woman) and is an excellent student, as well as, being a beautiful girl. Jody and Rebecca are doing an excellent job parenting Colleen. Jody has expressed to us what those years of visiting us in Kentwood meant to him. He has some very special memories from those days as a young boy. He recalls the butter pound cake that I made for him. He told me once how much he enjoyed the Wilkes Reunion where there were tables of good homemade dishes which included fried chicken, chicken pies, dressing, peas, butterbeans, etc. and every kind of dessert one could imagine.

As I was reading Jody's words of gratitude, it reminded me of the time that I took Patrick and Chris Wilkes to the Camp Moore Museum in Tangipahoa. Derry and I have always enjoyed having family and friends in our home.

The Wilkes family held the Lucion/Lavanda Wilkes Reunion each year in August—the hottest part of the summer in Louisiana. After the Lucion Wilkes children passed away, there was not the motivation to continue with the Wilkes Reunion. The Earl Wilkes family has approximately 100 members who get together occasionally for a Reunion.

Pam and Craig Forrest hosted one at their home in Kentwood at the end of December, 2012. The Earl/ Willie Wilkes family met during the Washington Parish Fair in October, 2013 in Janice Branch's yard next to the Fairgrounds. Most of the family attends the Fair each year which makes it an appropriate time to meet. Mother and Daddy were such good examples of showing love and hospitality to family and friends. This spirit of hospitality and love for family has been passed down to their children, grandchildren, and great-grandchildren.

Grandson Bill Johnson, Kellye, Mia, and Chase spent a week with Nita and Steve in Miami while Ross was home on spring break from Ave Maria University. One day Nita and Jennifer arranged for a time of tea with Kellye and Mia at the Orchid Festival at the Tropical Fairchild Gardens in Miami. We received a picture of Nita, Kellye, and Mia at the salon getting a pedicure. Another picture showed Mia at the American Girl Store purchasing a small American Girl doll which was a gift from "Mimi" Sttaudt. Her other grandmother "Nina" Johnson treated Mia's doll to a hair styling at the store. Nita and Jennifer are very creative and give a lot of thought in planning a social experience for others. Steve took Chase to the "Build a Bear" store where Chase built his first bear. They made trips to the beaches, swam daily in the Johnson pool, and enjoyed several days hanging out with the family. Bill and family left Miami Saturday evening to return to Nashville. Bill told his parents that he had had a real vacation of rest and relaxation. One cannot ask for anything more!

Derry and I attended the movie "Son of God" after taking a walk in the mall on Saturday. We highly recommend the movie which won some Academy Awards this year. I haven't cried that much in years. When we returned home, I walked to the mailbox to get the mail and spoke to my neighbor Salma who was cleaning out her car. She noticed that my eyes were red and asked me how I was doing. I explained to her that I had cried during the "Son of God" movie and still had red eyes.

Sunday, we walked again in the mall. Monday we walked the entire Lowe's store looking for a piece of duct board but failed to get it—didn't need to go to the mall to walk today. Monday evening, we went upstairs in our sitting room and watched the movie "Seabiscuit" that we thoroughly enjoyed. We took several boxes of our DVD's and VHS's upstairs to watch on other movie nights.

I had a nice telephone visit with Ms. Quettie who was my mother's best friend. She has been the leader in helping to get a grave marker placed on Aunt Vivian's grave. I am in the process of selecting and ordering a marker for her grave from Bogalusa Monuments.

Derry had quite a scare when the area under his right ear below the large incision to remove his squamous cell carcinoma in November made a large lump which really began to hurt him. Derry wanted to start with his dentist to rule out any problem with the teeth/jaw area. The dentist recommended that he contact the surgeon that removed the cancer. The surgeon's nurse stated that this lump has nothing to do with the surgical area. The surgeon sent him back to his dermatologist who sent him to the ENT doctor.

We made an appointment with Dr. Miller, ENT doctor at the new Scott/White Hospital three blocks from our house. He ordered an FNA (Fine Needle Aspiration) biopsy. We immediately called our Senior Pastor Troy Allen and our Youth Pastor Carey Todd and asked them to pray along with many of our family members and friends. The FNA did not reveal any cancer cells. *Praise God!* Derry will go in on Monday, March 31 at 9:30 for a CT scan. Our next step will be to have the lump removed. The lump causes him much discomfort. God is so good! Nita told her daddy, "Keep pulling those rabbits out of the hat."

We drove to north Bryan Saturday morning to watch David, Patrick's second son, play soccer. Due to his good athletic ability, he was assigned to a competition team which plays in Bryan each Saturday. Connor plays on a recreation team in Caldwell on Saturday. Pat and Jennifer are running back and forth from Caldwell to Bryan which is approximately 30 miles. We took our neighbor Sarah Hilal to her soccer practice last night while her mother went in another direction to take her son Yousef to his practice. Both practices meet at 7:00 p.m. Parents do a lot of running when their children participate in activities. Soccer is not the only activity that these children are involved in. I call Salma, the "Road Runner" transporting three children to various activities. I am sure Pat and Jennifer think that they are "Road Runners" also.

We were so pleased to hear that great-granddaughter Mia was awarded the Super Bear last nine weeks which is similar to an honor roll type achievement. Mia is extremely proud and excited. The family celebrated that night with gummy bears and teddy bear cookies.

Sunday, March 23, Derry and I drove to the Woodlands to join family and friends in the celebration of Doctors Fred and Nancy Thornberry's 50 years of marriage at the Bunch home which was hosted by their two daughters and sons-in-law: Michelle and Gordy Bunch and Molly and Thad Whisenant. The beautiful home was decorated with pictures and memorabilia of Fred and Nancy with tables of food, cake, and refreshments throughout the house. We enjoyed visiting with colleagues from TAMU and the College Station school district. On our way home, our good friend Bea Marin from Carrollton, TX called us. We were so pleased to hear from her and to hear how well her family members are doing.

Thank you for your prayers and concerns! God is so good! We are so blessed to be able to travel and participate with friends and family.

Journal April, 2014

Soccer practices and games for our great-nephews and neighbor began this month. The weather in the mornings was very windy and cool which made the environment a bit unpleasant. Another focus was the replacing of the iron fences around the lake behind our house. We did not actually assist with the fence building, but we allowed the contractor to use our driveway to bring in the new fence panels and take out the old panels through our driveway. This made an easier access for the fence contractor since the land around the lake was wet from rain. We got to know and respect Rick Ousley, owner of Iron Works, and his two Mexican workers. Since Rick and his crew were here on a daily basis, we asked him to give us a price to install an iron fence around our property. We agreed and contracted with him to build our fence. We wanted a fence that would keep our great-grandchildren and granddogs safe when they are visiting us and keep out wild hogs, armadillos, deer, and the ducks.

We began making preparation for our trip to Gatlinburg on April 18-25. We were kept busy making sure that we had all of

Derry's meds ordered, others purchased at CVS Pharmacy, and two weeks of med dispensers filled with his meds. We attended two of David's soccer games in Bryan but were not able to drive to Caldwell to see Conner's soccer game. Hopefully, we can see Conner play basketball or another sport when the weather warms. We did take Sarah Hilal to one of her soccer practices in College Station.

Derry went this month for blood work prior to seeing Dr. Bonds on April 11. Derry's blood pressure was good, heart in rhythm, cholesterol and glucose were good. Dr. Bonds examined the gland under his right ear that appeared sometime in January following his (MOS) squamous cell carcinoma procedure. After visiting several doctors in trying to find out what was going on, we finally visited Dr. Miller, ENT at Scott/White. He ordered a Fine Needle Aspiration and the results indicated that there were no cancer cells but there were some present. Doctors Simon and Miller scheduled Derry's surgery for April 29, the day after our return from TN and LA. Dr. Bonds instructed him to have it removed ASAP.

A rare treat for me was inviting a good friend to accompany me to tour the Parade of Homes sponsored by the Woman's Club of Bryan. We saw three of the most beautiful and recently built homes in the Traditions subdivision. Following the home tours, we enjoyed a lunch at Olive Garden. This was the second lunch that I have had with a friend since Derry's stroke on December 30, 2011. Since Derry's caregiver Mary was to leave at 1:00 p.m., Lee, Derry's former caregiver was not able to relieve Mary at 1:00 p.m., but her husband Wayne came and visited with Derry until I returned at 2:45 p.m. I have had the opportunity to eat lunch out many times, but I just could not do it alone. If I picked up a corn dog or small hamburger, I always came home to eat it. I just could not eat out without Derry.

We drove to New Orleans on April 17 to pick up Nita and Steve who accompanied us on our trip to Gatlinburg. I gladly turned over the driving to Steve and enjoyed sitting in the back seat with Nita. After leaving N.O., Steve remembered eating catfish at an old restaurant in downtown Slidell. Using his new telephone, he googled and found the directions to the restaurant.

After enjoying a fine meal, we drove to Meridian, MS where we spent the night. Friday, we drove Steve to Nashville so that he could attend Mia's softball game on Saturday. Nita drove us on to Gatlinburg to the Treetop Resort where we unloaded our luggage, ice chest, etc. and settled down for a good night's sleep. Saturday evening Bill and family with Steve drove to Gatlinburg where they spent the night and part of Sunday with us. Bill and family returned to Nashville to complete their Easter celebration with the Staudt's.

Monday, we spent the day at Dollywood which was the last day for the Festival of Nations. We especially enjoyed seeing the eagles in the preservation area up the side of the mountain within Dollywood. We drove through the Roaring Fork Motor Trail enjoying the beautiful scenery, rocks, streams, waterfalls, turkeys, etc. Nita and Steve went back the next day and explored the waterfalls. Derry and I enjoyed chilling out at the Resort and taking our short walks and sitting in the swing next to the creek enjoying the water flowing over the rocks. Nita and Steve spent one day enjoying Cherokee and climbing Clingman's Dome. Thursday, we toured Cade's Cove seeing many deer, bears, and turkeys.

Friday morning we packed up early and drove to sister Elaine's at Mt. Pisgah where we spent two nights and days. Luke and Tam Brooks brought their grandbaby Izie up to visit us. Luke promised us that he is coming to CS to see us. Saturday, we drove to Kentwood to visit Connie's Jewelry store and later ate delicious catfish at Nilah's in Osyka, MS. After lunch, we drove to Ponchatoula to visit Derry's sister and family. While there we picked three gallons of the sweetest strawberries that we shared with brother Chuck and Beck and brought Elaine two gallons. We drove down to the Wilkes farm and stopped by to see sister Faye who was recovering from a minor surgery.

Sunday morning we drove to N. O. and ate lunch at Olive Garden in the Esplanade Mall near the airport. We had coffee and Beignets at the Café Du Monde in the mall which does not provide the ambience that the French Quarter location does, but I was not going to put Derry through the ordeal of driving that far for a cup of coffee and the ambience. Derry was born in New

Orleans and lived there until he was 12. He does not share the joy and excitement of visiting there like others do. We dropped Nita and Steve off at the airport and drove to Baton Rouge where we spent the night.

Monday we drove to CS and arrived early enough to make final preparations with the nurse at the Scott/White Hospital for Derry's surgery on Tuesday morning on April 29. Dr. Miller removed a mass from the Perotid Gland that turned out to have squamous carcinoma cells in the mass which will require radiation after the body recovers from the surgery. We feel very blessed to have had Derry's surgery at the new Scott/White Hospital with four doctors taking care of him. Dr. Miller and Dr. Simon performed the surgery, but Dr. Miller assigned two hospitalists to take care of him through the night along with the excellent nurses. One hospitalist is a urologist and found a reason to call in Dr. Scott, urologist for a consultation. He found a small infection in Derry's prostrate which they began treating immediately.

Derry walked around the lake for exercise. He continues to have a walk each day whenever and wherever it is convenient. Our neighbors, Dr. and Mrs. Hilal, visited Derry and brought him a beautiful bouquet of flowers. Dr. Jordan, a surgeon at S/W and a friend and church member checked on us. His wife Kelly and children Wyatt and Weston came by for a visit with a basket of fruit. We could not be in a better place for meeting our needs. God is so good!

Journal May, 2014

As I told you in the previous journal, Derry had a mass removed from the Perotid Gland on April 29. Since he had several weeks to recover from the surgery, the doctor thought that it would be good for us to keep our plans to visit San Antonio. We enjoyed several days at the Wyndham LaCascada which is on the San Antonio River near the Riverwalk. We rode the River Cruise boat which was very educational and interesting. One day we caught the resort shuttle to San Antonio Market Place where we ate at the Mi Tierra Mexican restaurant. One day we ate at Ritas on the River. We made several walks which was the only exercise Derry could do until his incision healed. After doing these things that were on our bucket list, we were ready to come back to C.S.

Upon our return, we visited with Dr. Miller, ENT surgeon, who was pleased with Derry's healing. He informed us that as soon as the incision was healed, he would make arrangements for Derry to begin radiation therapy at the CS Med which is just across the interstate from our house. Derry visited with Dr. Bruce Hoekstra on May 8 and had some squamous cells removed from his face and hands. Dr. Hoekstra will keep a close watch on others as they appear and remove them immediately.

May 20 I began my dental journey with Dr. Williams. He made impressions to prepare for making new dentures that will be ready after the two implants on the bottom are healed and ready for the final procedure. My appointments begin the first week of June with Dr. Williams and Dr. Curtis Garrett.

Saturday, May 24 We joined the Schillings, Carey Todd our youth pastor and his family along with three girls from our church for a day of fun and relaxation at Linda and Walter Sensat's ranch at Burton. They are the parents of Carey's wife Brandi. The Sensat's had lunch with us at our home when Brandi had back surgery here in College Station at Scott/White.

Linda and Walter have a lovely home, small lake for swimming and fishing, a huge live oak tree that makes a great canopy for camping, and a neat bed/breakfast cottage setting near this huge oak tree. They served us brisket, beans, and all of the trimmings on a porch that surrounds their house. Connor, David, and Luke drove and rode the Mule over the farm all day. Kathryn (almost three) sat down by Walter under the shade and very dramatically stated twice with her arms stretched out, "I can't fish because someone has my pole." Patrick was baiting her hook and casting it into the water for her. It was a most relaxing and enjoyable day for all of us. They gave us a bag of freshly picked yellow squash—the best that we have had in a long time.

Tuesday, May 27 I took Derry to Dr. Hosea, podiatrist, in Bryan. That evening we went to Al and Ann Jones' farm west of Bryan for a Sunday School cookout. Al, as usual, cooked a delicious brisket and pork loin with the guests bringing side dishes and desserts. It was a delightful time of visiting and fellowshipping with our Christian friends whom we have known since 1990.

Wednesday, May 2, We saw Dr. David Scott, urologist, who had visited Derry late in the evening at S/W following his surgery and learned that he needed some treatment. This was a follow-up visit to see how the new medications were working for the urine retention. Derry has an appointment with him in July after some lab procedures.

Wednesday evening Thad Douglass, our summer youth intern, came to stay with us a couple of nights while working at the church with Carey. Thad will be back on June 20 to spend the remainder of the summer with us. He is a TAMU student who is in the Corps which was a good recommendation for us because we had not met him before. We enjoyed having him in our home for these two nights and look forward to him living in our home this summer.

Thursday morning, Derry and I along with Mary, his caregiver, began planting our new fig tree, a Turkey Brown variety, which will give us four fig trees in our yard. They say the Turkey Brown is a hardy fig tree. Derry stated, "We will see how hardy it is after our taking care of it." We don't have great "green thumbs" but have strengths in other ways. *Ha!*

We are excited that Derry's nephew-in-law, Shad and great niece Lauren will be staying with us June 11-13 while Lauren attends the 4-H Roundup at Texas A&M. I believe that Connor and David might be attending the Roundup.

Wishing you a great remainder of the summer! We do not look forward to the July and August weather in Texas. *It does get hot!*

Journal June/July, 2014

We began the month of June with making plans for extensive dental work for me and radiation treatments for Derry. I am only five minutes from my dentists' offices (Dr. Williams and Dr. Curtis Garrett). Derry's radiation treatments will be done by Dr. Bains whose office is in the CS Med, five minutes from our house. We are only five to ten minutes from all of our doctors in CS and Bryan.

Monday, I went in for a fitting of the model for top and bottom teeth. Dr. Andy Williams and his son Dr. Steven Williams, assessed the size and color of the teeth and placement of teeth. They wanted to make sure the midline was perfect. I took a 1957 picture of me smiling so that they would know what my teeth looked like when I had teeth. I go back on Wednesday, June 11, to see if any more adjustments need to be made. These teeth have to be made before I have my five remaining teeth pulled by Dr. Garrett and the two implants on the bottom inserted. I have a consultation on Monday, June 9 with Dr. Garrett for him to explain what he will do and when. I will begin tooth extractions and implants "planted" on September 4. He will insert my newly constructed teeth prepared by Dr. Williams.

It had been suggested that we check with our dentist to see how radiation would affect Derry's teeth. *I told my sister that Derry was the only one in the house who could chew a steak.* It would be a shame to lose those good teeth, but Dr. Bains reassured us that the radiation is not affecting the parotid gland on the left side. So far Derry has enough saliva being produced in his mouth to preserve his teeth. *Praise God!!*

After visiting with Dr. Bobby Bains, radiology oncologist, he assured us that he would do everything possible to minimize the area the radiation would reach. He spent several days working on the strategy to make this happen. Derry began his first treatment on Monday, June 23 and is doing well.

Dr. Bains reported to us that they are saving the left parotid gland during the radiation therapy which is a great blessing. Derry was experiencing some discomfort in his mouth where the radiation bounced off the metal fillings in his mouth and caused some irritation inside the mouth. Dr. Bains prescribed a special solution containing five different ingredients that a pharmacy in Bryan prepares for cancer patients. The solution is really making his mouth and throat better, allowing him to eat a hamburger patty last night with ease.

Dr. Miller was surprised that Derry's muscle in the right eye had not sprung back from the surgery and recommended that

Derry see his ophthalmologist to have it stitched. Dr. Perkins does not do this kind of surgery but sends patients to Austin. We were informed that Dr. Posvar with Scott and White does this kind of surgery at the SW local hospital. Dr. Bonds, Derry's primary doctor, made the referral for Derry to see Dr. Posvar on Monday, June 30 to make arrangements for the surgery. Doctors felt that his eye needed to be protected now, so Dr. Posvar performed Ectropion Repair Surgery on Wednesday, July 16. Derry had quite a bit of swelling in the eye area which did not allow the radiation mask to fit over the eye causing him to miss two days of radiation due to swelling.

Grandson Bill, Kellye, Mia, and Chase welcomed a new addition to their family with the arrival of Berkley Tate Johnson on June 30 in Nashville, TN. Steve, Nita, Jennifer, and Ross drove from Miami to be there several days for the delivery and to spend time with the Johnson family. We were not able to be there for this happy occasion due to scheduled radiation treatments for Derry. We look forward to a time when we can all be together.

We are very blessed to have our church's youth intern staying with us these five weeks. Thad Douglass is a Corps and band student at TAMU and exhibits all of the discipline and character building that TAMU's expects of their students. When Carey Todd, our youth minister, asked us if Thad could stay with us these six weeks, he stated that he was a Corps student at TAMU. I knew then that he would be a good match for two old people. While Thad was away a week attending camp with 46 young people, Derry surely did miss his coming in and out of the house.

Saturday night, June 21, Derry and I did not go to bed until nearly midnight. Derry took his sleep meds, put in his mouth guard to keep him from grinding his teeth, and I treated his eye and placed the two pillows to help support his left arm and hand. We were settled down to sleep, I thought. He began talking about several things and could not stop. Finally, he went into a deep sleep and had a wonderful dream. He dreamed that Mr. Sanders was running for a political office and Derry had agreed to go to Grangeville to make a picture of a wagon with six mules pulling the wagon in front of his great-grandfather Boley Bankston's house.

After telling me about the dream, Derry described to me that the front of Boley's house was at street level and the back of the house was on stilts that extended over the creek. When he was a very young person staying with great-grandfather Boley and grandmother Juanita Rivers Bankston, he remembered the goats sleeping under the house.

Sunday night, June 22, Derry went to bed as usual and went to sleep. After about five hours in the bed, he went to the kitchen to take another dose of his sleep meds. He reclined in the den recliner and went into a deep sleep. He dreamed about cousin Robin and Sue Burch who live on their Burch property next to the Silver Creek. In Derry's dream, Robin had built a long pipe that extended into the creek and the water pressure from the creek pushed the water up to his field. In this dream, Robin used this water for irrigating a field of grass where their cattle grazed. Their cows' milk production had dropped 27%, but was re-established when the cows grazed the irrigated grass. After telling me the dream, he stated, "I believe my brain is healing." *Praise God*! I have to agree with Derry. I have begun to notice that Derry does a better job of remembering to close car doors, outside doors, and turn off the water faucets. These things have been hard for him to remember to do. He has become much more talkative at times.

We began Derry's 80th birthday celebration on Saturday, July 5 with good friends, Gerald and Sandra Wynn and Lee and Wayne McNew, joining us for cake and ice cream. On Sunday, July 6, we prepared a meal after church for 16 family members and friends and acquaintances who attended. One of Derry's caregivers Mary helped me several days preparing for the meal and was here on Sunday to help with serving and cleaning up. Derry stated that the one thing missing in the celebration was that his daughter, son-in-law, grandchildren, and great-grandchildren were not present. We will have another 80th birthday celebration with only our family when they come for Christmas.

Ross has enjoyed his summer at home in Miami working, fishing, boating, spending time with friends, and working out at the gym in preparation for his football season at Ave Maria University. He is looking forward to being back at the university attending classes and playing football. Steve and Nita are making tentative plans to fly to College Station to drive Derry and me to Abilene Christian University, Abilene, TX, on October 11 for Ross' football game. We have not had the privilege of seeing Ross play football during his high school nor college years but plan to see him play before he graduates college. Traveling with Steve and Nita to see Ross play in Texas will be a real special time for us.

We plan to make a trip to Louisiana in September to attend my nephew Brody Wilkes' wedding. Brody is the younger son of Beck and Chuck Wilkes. We look forward to spending this special time with the family. My time is devoted each day taking care of Derry. My main focus is preparing foods that he can eat with his tender mouth.. Also, preparing foods for a diabetic, and one with high blood pressure and diverticulosis takes time in the grocery store and kitchen. With the help of caregivers four hours a day, we manage his care quite well.

Derry and I do not plan to do anything while he is in radation treatments except the necessary daily routine at home. We try to walk daily either in the supermarket, Walmart, Sam's, drug store, or down the long hall at the CS Med Center to get some exercise. Due to left-side weakness from the stroke in his left arm and hand, Derry is not strong enough to make required adjustments to the equipment at the new Aerofit gym; therefore, we cancelled the membership. After Derry completes his radiation treatments, we plan to join another gym that is better suited for seniors.

Due to so many of our church friends asking about Derry and his treatments, I sent the following e-mail to them and family.

"On Wednesday, when we met with the radiology oncologist, he told us that he was adding ten more treatments because Derry's body is tolerating the treatment very well. Derry's mouth and skin look very good. The left parotid gland is producing enough saliva to keep his mouth moist. Derry is faithful in carrying out the doctor's instructions for treating the mouth and skin. Dr. Bains stated that these additional ten treatments should be all that he will need. This will make a total of 40 treatments. Dr. Bains monitors Derry's weight each week as a measure of how his body is reacting to the treatments. Derry has only lost 4-5 pounds which pleased Dr. Bains. Patients are expected to lose two pounds per week. Keeping a close watch on his diet has much to do with this good outcome."

Derry's eye has recovered beautifully from the eye surgery in the midst of his continued radiation treatments. He is *one* strong man! He gives God the glory for where he is today on this medical journey.

Medical Update on Derry

In our last journal to you on January 3, 2015, we reported that Derry had completed a total of 79 radiation treatments and 7 chemo treatments for squamous cell carcinoma. One morning, Derry awoke with a very sore muscle in his neck—he thought. We rubbed it with Blu-Emu to help relieve the pain and discomfort. The next morning, as I was applying the ointment, I felt a knot in his neck. We immediately went in to see Dr. Miller who ordered a biopsy which came back malignant.

Dr. Miller (surgeon) and Dr. Bains (radiology oncologist) kept saying that they could not understand where this aggressive cancer cell came from because the treatments that had been performed consistently destroy a squamous cell carcinoma. Dr. Miller, Dr. Bains, and Dr. Rodriguez (chemo oncologist) continue to be perplexed about the origin of this cancer.

Upon the result of a previous PET scan, the radiologist commented that the kidney area "really lit up." The doctors wanted to know if the cancer cell had come from the kidneys. Derry shared with the doctors that he has known for about 15 years that he had multiple lesions in both kidneys. Dr. Cochran had sent the biopsy to four different labs to determine the prognosis. The Mayo Clinic was the fourth lab that found the lesions to be benign. A few years later, Dr. Cochran had another scan performed and could see very little change in the lesions and did not believe that there was anything to be concerned about.

Dr. Miller ordered two scans (one in the neck area and one in the chest area) that were done February 5 at S/W. Nephew Patrick took off work, drove us over to the clinic, and stayed with us until we were discharged to come home. Immediately following the infusion of the contrast, Derry felt his colon bleeding. Derry believed that he had had a reaction from the dye. After the bleeding continued for four days, we called Dr. Ragu's office and learned that he would be out of his office for 1 ½ weeks. We called Dr. Miller and asked if S/W had a GI doctor. He immediately scheduled an appointment for Derry within a day with Dr. Dusold. (Derry continued to believe that he had had an allergic reaction from the contrast during the CAT scans, but the doctors did not believe the dye was the cause of the bleeding.) After conferring with Dr. Dusold, we decided to give it another day or two to see if the bleeding would stop. The bleeding continued. Derry hemorrhaged for seven days from the colon passing large amounts of blood. His hemoglobin was 5.4. upon entering the hospital.

We were so excited that Nita came on Thursday to visit for a few days. She was such a blessing as an RN taking care of her daddy. She knew that he had been bleeding but was shocked to find him so low in blood. She began doing all that she knew to do to help at that time. After Derry went to bed, she and I visited for several hours about his condition. She went to bed, but I could not sleep. The Holy Spirit led me to begin making plans to get him to the hospital. I completely dressed and made preparations for going to the hospital. At 3:00 a.m., Derry went to the restroom. I told him that at 7:00 a.m., I would be calling 911, and he agreed. He went back to sleep. I went upstairs and told Nita what the plan was. At 7:00 a.m., I called 911. Before I could get Derry dressed, they arrived, put him on the stretcher, and away they went to Scott/White (three blocks from our house). Nita and I followed a few minutes later joining him in the radiology lab. The intervention radiologist performed a nuclear test and found out exactly where the blood was coming from without having to do a colonoscopy.

Dr. Banker (intervention radiologist) and Dr. Jordan (surgeon) had decided that Dr. Banker would perform the Lynx procedure, and if that did not work, Dr. Jordan would perform surgery to remove the part of the colon that was bleeding. Friday evening, Dr. Banker went through the femoral artery into the colon. He plugged up three arteries with the Mynx device which uses a soft, bio-absorbable, sponge-like sealant that absorbs blood and other fluids to seal the arteriotomy and stop the bleeding. *Amazing technology*!

Nita spent Friday and Saturday nursing Derry in the hospital. I engaged a caregiver to stay with him Saturday night from 10:00 p.m. until 6:00 a.m. so that Nita could get some rest and spend time with her aunts, three of my sisters who drove 500 miles from La. to spend several days with us. I did not tell my sisters that Derry was bleeding. They tried calling our house on Friday but could not get us. They knew something was going on.

Derry thoroughly enjoyed their visit even though he was in the hospital part of the time. As we anticipated Derry's coming home on Sunday, we all started preparing food for our family luncheon. Sunday morning, Nita and I went to the hospital to check on Derry. Nita stayed with him until he was discharged Sunday afternoon following the infusion of two more pints of blood, raising his Hemoglobin to 9.9. My sisters left Tuesday morning to drive back home. Nita left Tuesday afternoon to fly back to Miami.

Today, February 26, we went in to see Dr. Bains to get the results of the PET Scan done on Saturday at St. Joseph Lab. The report did not indicate that there was a problem with the kidneys. Dr. Bains expressed his disappointment and sadness about the failure to eradicate this cancer. We told him how much we appreciated what he had done. He raised the question. Could this cancer have come from a diverticulum in the colon? Derry has been plagued with diverticulosis for over 30 years. We just do not know at this point.

I told Dr. Bains that Derry and I read the Bible each day, praying and thanking God for his healing, and believe that God can and does perform miracles. He agreed that we are approaching the outcome in a very positive way. He asked that we keep him informed through his personal e-mail. He called Dr. Rodriguez and told him that he was referring Derry to him to see if there was anything that he could do. We are waiting to hear from Dr. Rodriguez.

Dr. McKernan, pain specialist, prescribed two drugs (Oxycodone and Gabapentin) that are helping Derry tolerate the pain caused by this growing cancer in the neck and chest area. We do not know what the final result will be, but we do know that Jesus can and does heal. We are asking that God's will be done. Regardless of the final outcome, *Derry is healed*!

Journal September/October, 2014

On August 28, we picked up our daughter Nita who flew into the Austin airport from Miami, FL. It was wonderful having her spend a few days with us. She accompanied us to the Scott/White Hospital on August 29 for Derry's follow-up appointment with Dr. Miller who performed his surgery removing the mass from the right perotid gland. Derry and Nita helped me celebrate my birthday by giving me a dozen beautiful red roses and cards. Nita flew back to Miami on Sunday, Aug. 30. Dr. Hoekstra froze some squamous cell growths from his skin on September 3.

I finally began the dental implants process on September 4 with Dr. James Garrett at 11:00 a.m. with several follow-up appointments for weeks that are required to check on gum healing and grafting around receptacles for implant posts. Dr. Williams over several months designed and had made my new teeth so that I could walk out with my new teeth after Dr. Garrett had installed the implants, but my mouth was not ready to wear these teeth. I reminded my dentist that he did not tell me that I would walk out with the teeth in a plastic bag. I will be eating soft foods until the middle of November.

On September 15, Derry had blood work done to prepare for a Cat Scan that was done on September 20 at the St. Joseph Cancer Center in Bryan. On September 22, Derry went for a visit with his cardiologist Dr. Schwartz for an Echo and exam. Dr. Schwartz was so excited that Derry was doing beautifully. Dr. Schwartz wished him Happy 80th birthday and is looking forward to his reaching 90 years old. As we shared some of the challenges that Derry is having with the cancer and colitis, he stated in jest,

"Boy, if these other doctors could do this well with you, you would certainly reach 90." Ha!

A Fun Time

ON THURSDAY, SEPTEMBER 25 we drove from CS and arrived in Ponchatoula to visit Derry's sister and brother-in-law for 1 ½ hours before driving to Elaine's for the night. On Friday, we visited Dora's family: Bobbie at her house, her son Craig and grandson at their home, Faye at her home, and Jan at her home in Franklinton. We visited the Burch Cemetery and Mt. Pisgah Cemetery where most of Dora's ancestors are buried. We wanted to see Aunt Vivian's grave marker that was placed by some family members. We met niece Beverly and husband at McDonald's where they gave their grandson his first ice-cream cone. Saturday, we attended nephew Brody Wilkes' wedding at FBC in Franklinton. That evening, Craig and Pam Forrest treated us and Elaine to a seafood dinner at Bo's. Sunday, we drove back to CS to get an early start on unpacking and doing laundry.

A Sad Time

TUESDAY, DORA HAD TWO DENTAL APPOINTMENTS for an assessment of dental work. Wednesday, October 1, Derry visited his podiatrist for his "pedicure." He went for lab work at S/White. October 2, Derry went to Bryan Radiology for an MRI. October 3, Dora had a bond density test and mammogram exam done at Bryan Radiology. At 2:40 p.m., we had our picture made for the church directory. October 6, Derry had lab work done at the Physician's Centre prior to Dr. Bonds visit on Wednesday. While there, the nurse gave Derry his pneumonia and flu shots.

Derry's MRI revealed that he had cancer in the lymph nodes under his right jaw and under the right collar bone which are being treated with chemo and radiation. Dr. Rodriguez, chemo oncologist, is using Erbetux, a targeted treatment, to weaken the cancer cells while Dr. Bains, radiology oncologist, is administering the radiology treatments to hopefully eradicate the cancer cells *forever*. Derry will have seven chemo treatments and 14 days + of radiation. We are very blessed that we live within two blocks of Scott/White Hospital where the chemo treatments are being administered and a few blocks from College Station Med where radiology treatments are being administered. We are doing all of the things prescribed to keep Derry's skin healthy following the chemo treatments. Also, his diet and the medicines prescribed to make his mouth more comfortable when eating helps with the chewing and swallowing.

Nita flew from Miami to New Orleans to spend several days with us at Elaine's lovely and comfortable home. We enjoyed spending time at my sister Jan's home three days where we met and greeted family and friends who stopped by while enjoying the Washington Parish Fair. We saw Jamie Lynn Spears, Brittany's sister perform on stage at the Fair.

Upon our return from Louisiana, we began meeting the doctor appointments that were previously made with Dr. Bains, Dr. Miller, Dr. Rodriguez, and Dr. Posvar. We are blessed to be less than ten minutes from any of these doctors.

Connor and David Schilling helped me put out sand to help fill up some low areas in the side yard where Derry walks to feed the birds. We finished just in time for the rain to slowly melt the sand into the grass. These two great nephews are old enough and well trained to work to help us do some things around the yard that we cannot do.

We are looking forward to having the Johnson family with us during the Christmas holidays. Continue to pray for Derry and pray specifically that his body will be totally healed from the cancer.

Journal November/December 2014

November was a busy month for us. Derry began a second round of radiation therapy for six weeks and seven weeks of chemo. Every day, Monday through Friday, Derry received a radiation treatment by Dr. Bobby Bains at the CS Medical Building. Each Friday, he received the Erbitux a targeted chemo treatment by Dr. Rodriguez at the new Scott/White Clinic/Hospital a few blocks from our house. We were blessed to have Dr. Hilal, our neighbor come to our home each Wednesday to flush Derry's PICC that had been inserted to eliminate the trauma of having to be stuck several times to insert a needle in his vein to get blood samples.

We had to have a new windshield installed due to a rock from somewhere hitting our windshield. The crack was too long to have it repaired. Safelite came to our house and installed the new one. It was very convenient to have them do the repair in our driveway.

We attended the Willie Nelson Concert held at the Rudder Auditorium on November 17. We were truly amazed that a man over 80 years could stand for nearly two hours playing his guitar and singing without ever sitting down. It was a very enjoyable experience for us.

I had to cancel my reservation to the BV Retired Teachers luncheon at Café Eccell due to the incompletion of my dental procedures. We are to start again in January to hopefully complete the implant process.

We enjoyed a visit by Dr. Allen Roussel and Dr. Dan Posey from the LAMS Hospital who are former colleagues of Derry. I served them coffee and pie. Derry and I attended the CVM Retired Faculty Luncheon held at the new Equine facility hosted by Dean Green. One of Derry's classmates who made his money as a lawyer donated $35 million to build this Equine facility which is named for him. Dr. Green is an incredibly intelligent woman. She is a veterinarian, a leader, a planner, and a motivator. She has helped bring in millions of dollars to build a new small animal hospital and state of the art classroom facility. It is so important that Derry remain a part of this CVM and TAMU community where he dedicated 17 years as a clinical associate professor in the Large Animal Medicine and Surgery, CVM at TAMU.

Thanksgiving was a quiet day for us so that we could begin making preparations for a BIG Christmas celebration in anticipation of our family coming from Miami and Nashville for a week. A week before Christmas Steve, Nita, Jennifer, and Ross drove from Miami, FL and Bill, Kellye, Mia, Chase, and Berkley drove from Nashville, TN.

During Christmas week, we celebrated Derry's 80th birthday again so that he would have his family with him in this celebration. He stated on July 5th when we gave him an 80th birthday party that he would be 80 all year long and wanted a party with his three great-grandchildren. Sandee's Sweets designed and made the cake according to Derry's instructions decorating the vanilla cake in primary colors for the children. Sandy delivered his cake on Friday, December 26. The cake included the names and ages of Mia-7, Chase-4, and Berkley-6 months, Derry's 80th, and our 62 years of marriage.

Derry celebrates his 80th birthday with great-grandchildren.

Mia helped her mother Kellye and me purchase the cow plates, napkins, cups, and balloons for Derry's celebration that he had looked forward to for months. As he sat in front of the cake, he was surrounded by Mia and Chase with Berkley in his lap while the family looked on. We did not mind that her toe touched the icing on the cake. After all, it was her cake, too. We thank our family for making the effort to travel the long distances to make this Christmas week very special. We will look forward to planning his 90th birthday. Dr. Schwartz, his cardiologist, tells him each visit that he plans to see him reach his 90th birthday.

On Friday, we were honored to have Steve's aunt Mina from Dallas come and spend the day with us. She is such a beautiful woman inside and out. I have known Aunt Mina since she attended Steve and Nita's wedding in 1972 in Kentwood, LA. She is a very dedicated aunt who attends all of the families' events regardless of the distance. I was very honored in 2012 to be her guest at the Brazos Valley Christian Women's luncheon at Pebble Creek Country Club where she was the guest speaker. She gave her Christian testimony which is an incredible story of how God has worked in her life. She is a professional singer and has made recordings of Christian music that she shares with churches throughout Texas. We are praying that she will come back and spend several days with us.

Following the luncheon that day in 2012, Aunt Mina accompanied me to the St. Joseph Rehab to visit Derry who was not able to stand or walk at that time. She was so amazed to see him now and enjoyed visiting with him. They talked about her and Steve's family tree which was included in our book.

Derry and I attended the Christmas Luncheon at the LAMS Department where we enjoyed delicious fried frog legs and fried quail which was part of the menu requested by Dr. Allen Roussel, a Louisiana native who is the LAMS Department Head. The frog legs and quail were shipped in from South Louisiana by the caterer. The luncheon included steak smothered in gravy along with other side dishes and multiple desserts. The real value to attending this luncheon is for Derry to meet and greet the faculty and staff that he enjoyed working with for 17 years. This is one of the benefits from retiring in CS along with the medical staff and medical facilities.

Both Johnson families returned to their homes. The Nashville Johnsons returned home on Saturday/Sunday to begin making plans to take children to the doctor. The Steve Johnsons with their two dogs began their drive back to Miami on Sunday with a night stay in Pensacola. They arrived home on Monday evening. They began preparing for Steve to smoke a turkey for their New Year's Day dinner. Nita makes an awesome turkey gumbo with the carcus and trimmings. The gumbo will be delayed because Nita received a call from the Nurse Traveling Agency requesting that she fly to Salt Lake City on Friday to assist transporting a patient from the hospital in SLC to New York. This patient refuses to fly; therefore, he arranged for two nurses and two drivers to drive him in a motor home from Salt Lake City to New York. We know Nita will enjoy seeing the sights along the way while nursing the patient.

As I was working in the office Friday evening, we received a call from grandson Ross who was traveling with a buddy from Naples, FL to Panama City Beach to attend the wedding of one of Ross' college roommates. About two hours from Panama City Beach, they learned that the house that they had been invited to stay in was not available. Ross made his dad aware of their dilemma and Steve suggested to Ross that he call us to see if we could check with Wyndham to see if they had a room available near the church in Panama City Beach. Using our Wyndham Reward Points, I got them a room at the Hawthorne which was 1.3 miles from the church where the wedding was taking place. After Ross and his buddy arrived at the Hawthorne, he called excitedly to say how fabulous the room was: two queen-size beds, a kitchen, walk-in closet, and a free complete continental breakfast Saturday morning. (I hope the hotel breakfast room had *plenty* of food.)

Ross and his buddy were waiting for a friend to come pick them up to ride dune buggies on the beach. Ross called us Saturday afternoon to thank us again for the nice accommodations and reported that they were not able to do the dune buggy rides due to the holidays, but they found a bumper car facility open. Derry and I feel honored and overjoyed in having a part in our grandchildren's lives.

Even though Derry has completed his radiation and chemo treatments, he has been left with the consequences of these treatments. The Erbitux treatments caused blisters and sores throughout his body. When Dr. Rodriguez saw the breaking out on Derry's body he responded, "It's working!" Derry's chest and shoulder areas were so burned by the radiation that Dr. Bains cancelled the last treatment. Derry is being the strong man that he is by trying to "grin and bear it." He is constantly doing things to help relieve the pain and discomfort. Praise God for Derry's tenacity and fortitude. His appetite is good which has helped him maintain his weight.

We were blessed by the kindnesses shown to our family by friends, family, and neighbors who brought by or mailed to us an array of Holiday goodies for us to enjoy.

Derry fought for his life to the bitter end.

WE KEPT PRAYING AND BELIEVING THAT GOD would heal Derry, but Derry was healed when God took him to Heaven. He passed away on June 3, 2015 at our home in College Station, TX in the presence of our family. We began immediately planning a Memorial Service in College Station, TX where we had lived over 20 years. We arranged for a second funeral in Kentwood, Louisiana where we had lived for 32 years. He was buried next to his father and mother in the Line Creek Cemetery north of Kentwood, LA.

Derry's Obituary

July 5, 1934 – June 3, 2015
Dr. Derry David Magee, D.V.M. died at the age of 80 at his home in College Station, Texas on Wednesday, June 3, 2015 at 3:18 p.m. He was born on July 5, 1934 in New Orleans, LA to Marvin Mangum Magee and Mary Bridges Magee. Derry married Gwendora Wilkes Magee on October 11, 1952 at Mt. Hermon, LA. He graduated Mt. Hermon High School in 1952; received his pre-veterinary education at Louisiana State University and Doctor of Veterinary Medicine at Texas A&M College of Veterinary Medicine in 1958.

Upon graduation from Texas A&M, Derry opened a veterinary practice in Tangipahoa Parish, LA; first in Amite, LA and later in Kentwood, LA where he practiced for 32 years. In 1990, he joined the Large Animal and Medicine Department in the College

103

of Veterinary Medicine at Texas A&M University serving as a Clinical Associate Professor for 17 years and serving as Staff Veterinarian for the Texas Department of Criminal Justice. His life's passion was veterinary medicine having set the goal to become a veterinarian at age 12. His life carried out the scripture found in Proverbs 16:9 "In his heart a man plans his course, but the LORD determines his steps." His 49 years as a practicing veterinarian were spent in finding ways to help farmers reach success in their operations and teaching and encouraging students at LSU and TAMU to reach their goals.

Derry enjoyed spending time with his family and friends. After retiring in 2007, he began researching and writing his family history and genealogy. He enjoyed reading, fishing, sports, and studying the Bible. Derry served as a deacon and Bible teacher at First Baptist Church of Kentwood, LA and First Baptist Church of College Station, TX. He was a member of the Masonic Lodge of Kentwood, LA. He was a recipient of the American Farmers Degree in FFA;-high school valedictorian;-Borden's Award at LSU with highest GPA in the School of Agriculture; and graduated 7th in his veterinary medicine class at Texas A&M with honors.

Derry is survived by his wife, Gwendora "Dora", of 62 years; daughter, Juanita Magee Johnson and husband, Steven W. Johnson of Miami, FL.; grandchildren, Jennifer Jean Johnson, William Derry "Bill" Johnson and wife Kellye, and Ross Melvin Johnson; great-grandchildren, Mia Mckenzie Johnson, William Chase Johnson, and Berkley Tate Johnson. Also surviving is his sister, Mary Jane Fabre and husband Noland Fabre Jr.; nieces Melody Fabre Howes and Dr. Robin Fabre Ellison and husband Shad Ellison; nephew, Noland "Jody" Fabre III and wife Rebecca; great-nephews, John Howes and Joshua Ellison; and great-nieces, Lauren Ellison and Colleen Fabre.

He was preceded in death by his parents, Rev. Marvin Mangum Magee and Mary Bridges Magee; brother, Marvin Mangum Magee, Jr.

Funeral service will be 11:00 a.m. Saturday June 6 at Memorial Funeral Chapel in College Station with Rev. Troy Allen officiating. Visitation will be one hour prior to service time at the funeral home. A second funeral service will be held 11:00 a.m. Tuesday June 9 at Line Creek Baptist Church in Kentwood, LA. Visitation will be one hour prior to service time at the church. Interment will follow at Line Creek Cemetery.

In lieu of flowers, the family requests that gifts in memory of Dr. Magee be directed to the Dr. Derry Magee Scholarship Fund. Checks should be made payable to the Texas A&M Foundation and mailed to the College of Veterinary Medicine, Attn: Dean's Office, 4461 TAMU, College Station, TX 77843-4461.

Memorial Services

College Station Memorial Service

Dr. Derry David Magee Service in College Station , Texas
June 6, 2015
Officiated by Bro. Troy Allen
Visitation 10:00 a.m. — Service 11:00 a.m.

Congregational	"Count Your Many Blessings"
Cary Todd	Scripture, Prayer, Obituary
Patrick Schilling	Revelation 21:2-4; 2Corinthians 5:6-8
Quartet	"Great Is Thy Faithfulness"

Remembrances of grandfather (DeeDee)

Jennifer Johnson	John 14:1-2
Bill Johnson	Psalms 63:1,7
Ross Johnson	Psalms 18:1-3; Psalms 16:9-11

Quartet   "In the Garden"

Remembrances of father and father-in-law (Daddy and Doc)

Gwendora Magee

Juanita Magee Johnson   2 Timothy 4:6-8
Steven Winslow Johnson   Psalms 34:19; Psalms 15:1-2: Luke 23:43

Rev. Troy Allen   Message   (Job 1:1)

Rick Mitchell   Scripture/Prayer
Congregational   "I'll Fly Away"

Pallbearers: William Derry "Bill" Johnson   Cary Todd
              Ross Melvin Johnson   Thad Douglass
              William Patrick Schilling   Wesley Wynn

Honorary Pallbearers: Gerald Wynn
              Dr. Khaled Hilal   Monte Carmichael
              Dr. Troy Simon   Tom Gibbs
              Dr. Jim Anderson   Don Landry
              Dr. Wendell Horne   Allen Lea
              Gen. Tom Darling   Gene Bickham
              Dr. Robert Sanders   Walter Schuster
              Jimmy Bond   Jerry Estep

The family would like to express their appreciation to Comfort Keepers, Traditions Health Care, and Scott & White doctors and staff for providing comfort and medical care for Derry during his illness. We say thanks to the pastors, staff, Cornerstone Class, and church members of First Baptist Church of College Sstation, TX for their expressions of love through visits, phone calls, and cards. We give a special thanks to our neighbors who were always available when needed.

Service conducted by Memorial Funeral Chapel

Dr. Derry David Magee Memorial Service
College Station, Texas
Saturday, June 6, 2015 at 11:00 A.M.
Officiated by Rev. Troy Allen

Derry Magee Job 1: 1 *"In the land of UZ there lived a man whose name was Job. This man   was blameless and upright; he feared God and shunned evil."*

Derry Magee was my friend.

- Derry's handshake was firm and solid. One can tell a lot about a man by it. The handshake was the way a deal was made and that was good enough. It was a reflection of his honesty and the way he did business.
- Student/Teacher—Like Paul, Derry was a student and teacher. He was a pioneer and innovator in veterinary medicine. He spent his time learning, reading, developing, improving, and always thinking. The best teachers do!
- Derry taught more outside the classroom than in it. He was a hands-on teacher—not just in veterinary medicine but in life.
- Derry's heart for teaching came from his heart for learning. In Louis L'Amour's book, <u>Education of a Wandering Man</u>, he writes, *"I think the greatest gift anyone can give to another is the desire to know, to understand. Life is not for simply watching spectator sports or for taking part in them; it is not for simply living from one working day to the next. Life is for delving, discovering, learning."*
- Derry made an investment in the lives of his students and genuinely cared for them.
- Derry was faithful. There was no *quit in him.* He had perseverance, grit, was consistent—always knowing what you got with Derry—no pretense. Counted on seeing him in Sunday and Wednesday services
- Derry was honest. I loved to hear him pray—not eloquent but honest and true—from the heart.
- Derry was a good neighbor. (Recognized Khaled and Salma as an example.) This was a picture of how the Bible defines a neighbor. Luke 10: 29-31*But he wanted to justify himself, so he asked Jesus, "And who is my neighbor?" In reply Jesus said: "A man was going down from Jerusalem to Jericho, when he fell into the hands of robbers. They stripped him of his clothes, beat him and went away, leaving him half dead. A priest happened to be going down the same road, and when he saw the man, he passed by on the other side."* In verse 33, *"But a Samaritan, as he traveled, came where the man was; and when*

he saw him, he took pity on. He went to him and bandaged his wounds...."A good neighbor is one who cares for others.

- Derry was respected. One could not help but respect him. He was respectful, honorable, dignified, true Southern gentleman.
- Family was very important to Derry. He loved them all. They were one of the great joys of his life. He was proud of who you are and what you have become and are becoming. His family extended beyond just his own but even to mine. When I was visiting in Derry and Dora's home, I shared with them that I would be working on my doctorate, and they were excited for me. As I was leaving, Derry walked me to the door and stated, "Troy, I am happy that you are working on your doctorate, but DO NOT NEGLECT YOUR FAMILY."

Friend. Many are lucky to have one/two good friends. If Derry was yours, you were the lucky one. Derry had many good friends, colleagues but so much more.

Derry was all of these things not to earn favor with God but because God lived within him. Jesus was his Savior and His work showed through Derry. Why? Job 1:1

Blameless—Because of the work of Jesus in him.

Righteous—May not have always been right, but he always did right because of Jesus in him.

Feared God—Revered God because he loved God. Derry's favorite Bible character was King David who loved God and was a man after God's own heart. So was Derry.

Proverbs 16:8 *"The heart of man plans his way, but the Lord establishes his steps."* This scripture depicts how Derry lived his life.

Joy in the Journey

Line Creek Memorial Service

DERRY DAVID MAGEE'S SERVICE AT LINE CREEK BAPTIST CHURCH
WITH

McKneely Funeral conducting the burial

Tuesday, June 9, 1915

(Family Viewing at 9:30 a.m., public viewing at 10:00 a.m. and Service
at 11:00 a.m. with burial at Line Creek Cemetery)

ORDER OF SERVICE

Congregational Song	"Count Your Many Blessings"
Dick Day	Scripture, Prayer, Obituary
Patrick Schilling	Revelation 21:2-4: 2 Corinthians 5:6-8
Quartet	"Great Is Thy Faithfulness"
Jennifer Johnson	John 14:1-2
Bill Johnson	Psalms 63:1,7
Ross Johnson	Psalms 18:1-3; Psalms 16:9-11
Congregational Song	"Give Me That Old Time Religion"
Steve Johnson	Psalms 34:19; Psalms 15:1-2; Luke 23:43
Nita Johnson	2 Timothy 4:6-8
Bill Morris	Eulogy
Dick Day	Message
Dick Day	"Were It Not for Grace"
Quartet	"I'll Fly Away"

Letter from Bill Morris

Lancaster, South Carolina

Saturday, March 6, 2015

Dear Derry,

Growing up in Kentwood, Line Creek and Mount Hermon were not that far away, and Brother Marvin was larger-than-life. I knew who Derry Magee was, for I had watched him play basketball in the Kentwood gym.

Then in 1964 things changed. It's been 51 years that you and I have been dear friends. The first 25 years or so we saw each other several times a week and in some cases several times a day. Velta tells that Dora was the first person to come see her when we moved above the store in 1964. Art was just a baby. It was the same year Dr. Keller came to work with you. If I remember right, Nita was a preteen or an early teenager at best.

You were with us at the apartment over the store, and you were with us when we moved to the country on *4 Acres*. You were a very real presence in the life of our boys, and you were there for every major milestone of their lives. You were there for their graduations from both high school and college and attended both their weddings. You have been very real to our daughters-in-law, Merritt and Karen. I suppose, Derry, what I'm trying to say is *thank you* for being a very positive influence on all of my family and me.

We talked business—the trials and tribulations thereof. We've talked church—the trials and tribulations of it, and we did life together. Along the way, we experienced life with others. I'll just name two couples: Don and Barbara Bearden and Jim and Linda Headrick. Both men were called to glory way too soon for me, but the Lord knows best. Along the way, you have opened your arms to our kinfolk to name one, Butch. You and Butch laughed and worked together, and you were with him in a very tragic time in his life. Thank you for loving Butch.

You knew my financial struggles from the very beginning. I shared with you more about our family's financial struggles than with anyone on this earth. I've always known I could share anything with you. You knew when I came to South Carolina to interview for a job. Outside of Velta, Daddy and Connie, you were the first person I talked to about taking the job up here, and I don't remember your exact words, but the essence of the conversation was "Take the job Bill." Little did I know then, that in just over a year, you would move to College Station. It was in 1989 or 1990 that on one of my trips to College Station, you and I had dinner at Red Lobster. Dora was still in Kentwood. And for these last 25+ years, you have been in College Station, and I have been in South Carolina. We didn't see each other every day or every week, but we followed each other's progress. You continue to keep up with my boys. Thank you!

The future for both of us is uncertain, but we both hold on to our faith and what Jesus did for us on the cross, that same Jesus your dad preached about for so many years.

If our trip to see you doesn't work out, please know that you have been a big part of my life, and I thank you. One day in glory, which I have no idea what it'll be like, we can talk about all these things. I'll go fishing with you in that lake full of bass God has provided for you in his eternal kingdom.

Blessings to you and Dora!

I love you,

Bill

Louisiana Service for Dr. Derry David Magee

June 9, 2015

"When Grace and Death Collide"

Ralph Waldo Emerson said, "Life is a journey, not a destination."

Recently, Libby and I have had a couple of mixed events in our travels that centered around our oldest granddaughter. We attended her graduation at Texas A&M, visited with Derry and Dora, and afterward drove to Austin to visit Libby's first cousin and attended church with them. On occasions like these, we want to blend in, dressing appropriately. But with the unknown, as we had not attended an A&M graduation before and did not know if church was coat and tie or more casual as many churches are today, so we packed for the journey with different options.

Back in April, we met our son and family in Las Vegas. Because we were flying, taking everything in the closet was not an option. Because we are not seasoned flyers, we tended to fret more about putting a wardrobe together. Two weekends ago that same granddaughter got married. Our son who is a seasoned flyer showed up with a single carry-on and a backpack for the wedding and dress-up rehearsal supper. We had put a clothes bar in the car to hold all of our clothes. So, it is with this journey called "life." We often pack more than we need trying to anticipate events we have no control over.

Corrie Ten Boom tells this story in her book about her father. He stated, "Corrie, when you and I go to Amsterdam, when do I give you your ticket?" "Why, just before we get on the train." "Exactly. And our wise Father in Heaven knows when we're going to need things too. Don't run out ahead of Him. When the time of need comes, you will look into your heart and find the strength you need—just in time."

Corrie, later in life, after the concentration camp, Corrie wrote, "God will give us the grace and power we need—the money for the train ticket will arrive just the moment we are to step on the train."

Because we are but travelers, only pilgrims on our journey through life, knowing that our final destiny is with God, we keep our sight always fixed, not just on the appearance of this life but on the fact that we were created by God. We cannot be truly happy unless we live as God wishes us to live, and of course, God wants only what is good for us. We keep our eyes fixed on the fact that our destiny is eternal life and not just death.

As we become seasoned travelers on our life's journey, we tend to carry less baggage. In these last few weeks, God has given to Dora and family grace and power in their time of need.

Last Wednesday, Derry slipped through that door called death. You will remember the movie, *"Field of Dreams,"* where James Earl Jones, who played the part of a reporter, walked toward the corn field and tentatively reached out his hand into the field and then withdrew it. We do not get that opportunity. You see eternity has a door, and death is that door. It is the door of no return. Beyond that door, there are no second chances.

On our trip to Vegas, we took a trip to the Grand Canyon. We came back and told our friends that we had seen the Grand Canyon, but what we really saw was a small part of the Grand Canyon. So, it is with life. We see only small segments at a time.

In Derry's life, each of shared segments of his life. As in our case, that segment started in 1964 when I was called to FBC at Kentwood, La. as their Minister of Music. The time together was brief, but the bond that Libby and I have with Derry and Dora has lasted 50 plus years.

Was Derry ready to step through that door called *death,* and, if so, what prepared him for that step?

Fanny Crosby in the hymn, *"Amazing Grace,"* tells us that though we have *"toils and snares"* in life, *"Tis grace that has brought us safe thus far and grace will lead us home."*

Paul wrote in Ephesians 2:8 *"by grace are ye saved through faith, and that not of yourselves, it is the gift of God."* If we were to look up the word in Webster Dictionary, we would see that grace is the *"unmerited divine assistance given man for his regeneration or sanctification."* So grace is favor, *"unmerited favor."*

At an early age Derry received this *"unmerited favor"* of God when he placed his trust in Jesus. Salvation is of divine origin. But it is not anything that God was bound to arrange by the necessity of His nature. It is the result of His gracious will. Had it not been for His good pleasure, salvation would never have come. *"By grace are ye saved."* Salvation is a gift; it is not earned.

With this new life that God gave Derry came a new direction. Did Derry know all that God had planned for him? Of course not, but the important thing is God knew and one day He would bring him home. At each stage of Derry's life, God gave him the *"ticket"* for each phase of his journey. It is only when we look back at our life do we come to realize the words of Proverbs 16:9 (ESV) *The heart of man plans his way, but LORD establishes his steps."*

We have heard in Bill's Eulogy some of the details of Derry's life. As he aged, he came to that door of death. I have outlined that he was not alone on the journey of life but had a faithful guide that dwelt within another *"gift of God,"* the Holy Spirit.

But what took place once Derry stepped through that door? The church at Corinth also had this concern. What happened after death? Paul would write to them in I Corinthians 15:35-38—*But someone may ask, "How will be dead be raised? What kind of bodies will they have?" 36 What a foolish question! When you put a seed into the ground, it doesn't grow into a plant unless it dies first. 37 And what you put in the ground is not the plant that will grow, but only a bare seed of wheat or whatever you are planting. 38 Then God gives it the new body he wants it to have. A different plant grows from each kind of seed. 39 Similarly, there are different kinds of flesh—one kind for humans, another for animals, another for birds, and another for fish. 40 There are also bodies in the heavens and bodies on the earth. The glory of the heavenly bodies is different from the glory of the earthly bodies. 41 The sun has one kind of glory, while the moon and stars each have another kind. And even the stars differ from each other in their glory. 42 It is the same way with the resurrection of the dead. Our earthly bodies are planted in the ground when we die, but they will be raised in glory. 43 Our bodies are buried in brokenness, but they will be raised in glory. They are buried in weakness, but they will be raised in strength. 44 They are buried as natural human bodies, but they will be raised as spiritual bodies. For just as there are natural bodies, there are also spiritual bodies.*

The scriptures tell us, 45 *"The first man, Adam, became a living person." But the last Adam—that is, Christ—is a life-giving Spirit. 46 What comes first is the natural body, then the spiritual body comes later. 47 Adam, the first man, was made from the dust of the earth, while Christ, the second man, came from heaven. 48 Earthly people are like the earthly man, and heavenly people are like the heavenly man. 49 Just as we are now like the earthly man, we will someday be like the heavenly man. 50 What I am saying, dear brothers and sisters, is that our physical bodies cannot inherit the Kingdom of God. These dying bodies cannot inherit what will last forever. 51 But let me reveal to you a wonderful secret. We will not all die, but we will all be transformed! 52 It will happen in a moment, in the blink of any eye, when the last trumpet is blown. For when the trumpet sounds, those who have died will be raised to live forever. And we who are living will also be transformed. 54 Then, when our dying bodies have been transformed into bodies that will never die, this Scripture will be fulfilled: Death is swallowed up in victory. 55 O death, where is your victory? O death, where is your sting?" 56 For sin is the sting that results in death, and the law gives sin its power. 57 But thank God! He gives us victory over sin and death through our Lord Jesus Christ. 58 So, my dear brothers and sisters, be strong and immovable. Always work enthusiastically for the Lord, for you know that nothing you do for the Lord is ever useless.*

Paul also told the church at Thessalonica—1 Thessalonica 4:13 *And now, dear brothers and sisters, we want you to know what will happen to the believers who have died so you will not grieve like people who have no hope. 14 For since we believe that Jesus died and was raised to life again, we also believe that when Jesus returns, God will bring back with him the believers who have died. 15 We tell you this directly from the Lord: We who are still living when the Lord returns will not meet him ahead of those who have died. 16 For the Lord himself will come down from heaven with a commanding shout, with the voice of the archangel, and the trumpet call of God. First, the Christians who have died will rise from the graves. 17 Then together with them, we who are still alive and remain on earth will be caught up in the clouds to meet the Lord in the air. Then we will be with the Lord forever. 18 So encourage each other with these words.*

"Encourage one another with these words."

Funerals are for the living so we can reflect on the life our loved one but also to be encouraged that we will see them again.

Earlier I had said that Libby and I have enjoyed a bond with Derry and Dora for 50 plus years. I used word *have* instead of *had a bond* because we will see Derry again and though our space is altered our bond remains. He is one of those *who has gone before.* The *grace of God* which is His Son Jesus has kept Him safe and has brought him home.

Solo by Rev. Dick Day—*"Were It Not For Grace"*

PALL BEARERS

William Derry "Bill" Johnson
Ross Melvin Johnson
Earl S. Wilkes
Patrick Schilling
Dr. Card E. Keller

Pedigree Chart - Mia Mckenzie Johnson

15 March 2013

Chart no. _____
No. 1 on this chart is the same as no. _____ on chart no. _____

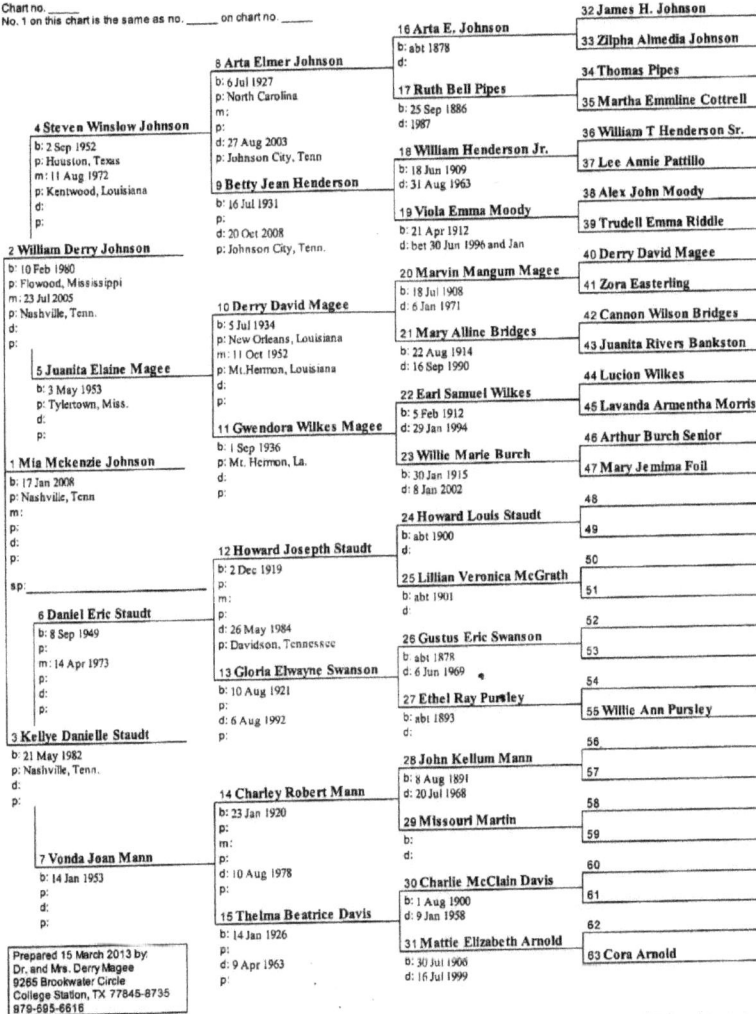

4 Steven Winslow Johnson
b: 2 Sep 1952
p: Houston, Texas
m: 11 Aug 1972
p: Kentwood, Louisiana
d:
p:

2 William Derry Johnson
b: 10 Feb 1980
p: Flowood, Mississippi
m: 23 Jul 2005
p: Nashville, Tenn.
d:
p:

5 Juanita Elaine Magee
b: 3 May 1953
p: Tylertown, Miss.
d:
p:

1 Mia Mckenzie Johnson
b: 17 Jan 2008
p: Nashville, Tenn
m:
p:
d:
p:

sp:

6 Daniel Eric Staudt
b: 8 Sep 1949
p:
m: 14 Apr 1973
p:
d:
p:

3 Kellye Danielle Staudt
b: 21 May 1982
p: Nashville, Tenn.
d:
p:

7 Vonda Joan Mann
b: 14 Jan 1953
p:
d:
p:

8 Arta Elmer Johnson
b: 6 Jul 1927
p: North Carolina
m:
p:
d: 27 Aug 2003
p: Johnson City, Tenn

9 Betty Jean Henderson
b: 16 Jul 1931
p:
d: 20 Oct 2008
p: Johnson City, Tenn.

10 Derry David Magee
b: 5 Jul 1934
p: New Orleans, Louisiana
m: 11 Oct 1952
p: Mt.Hermon, Louisiana
d:
p:

11 Gwendora Wilkes Magee
b: 1 Sep 1936
p: Mt. Hermon, La.
d:
p:

12 Howard Josepth Staudt
b: 2 Dec 1919
p:
m:
p:
d: 26 May 1984
p: Davidson, Tennessee

13 Gloria Elwayne Swanson
b: 10 Aug 1921
p:
d: 6 Aug 1992
p:

14 Charley Robert Mann
b: 23 Jan 1920
p:
m:
p:
d: 10 Aug 1978
p:

15 Thelma Beatrice Davis
b: 14 Jan 1926
p:
d: 9 Apr 1963
p:

16 Arta E. Johnson
b: abt 1878
d:

17 Ruth Bell Pipes
b: 25 Sep 1886
d: 1987

18 William Henderson Jr.
b: 18 Jun 1909
d: 31 Aug 1963

19 Viola Emma Moody
b: 21 Apr 1912
d: bet 30 Jun 1996 and Jan

20 Marvin Mangum Magee
b: 18 Jul 1908
d: 6 Jan 1971

21 Mary Alline Bridges
b: 22 Aug 1914
d: 16 Sep 1990

22 Earl Samuel Wilkes
b: 5 Feb 1912
d: 29 Jan 1994

23 Willie Marie Burch
b: 30 Jan 1915
d: 8 Jan 2002

24 Howard Louis Staudt
b: abt 1900
d:

25 Lillian Veronica McGrath
b: abt 1901
d:

26 Gustus Eric Swanson
b: abt 1878
d: 6 Jun 1969

27 Ethel Ray Pursley
b: abt 1893
d:

28 John Kellum Mann
b: 8 Aug 1891
d: 20 Jul 1968

29 Missouri Martin
b:
d:

30 Charlie McClain Davis
b: 1 Aug 1900
d: 9 Jan 1958

31 Mattie Elizabeth Arnold
b: 30 Jul 1906
d: 16 Jul 1999

32 James H. Johnson
33 Zilpha Almedia Johnson
34 Thomas Pipes
35 Martha Emmline Cottrell
36 William T Henderson Sr.
37 Lee Annie Pattillo
38 Alex John Moody
39 Trudell Emma Riddle
40 Derry David Magee
41 Zora Easterling
42 Cannon Wilson Bridges
43 Juanita Rivers Bankston
44 Lucion Wilkes
45 Lavanda Armentha Morris
46 Arthur Burch Senior
47 Mary Jemima Foil
48
49
50
51
52
53
54
55 Willie Ann Pursley
56
57
58
59
60
61
62
63 Cora Arnold

Prepared 15 March 2013 by:
Dr. and Mrs. Derry Magee
9265 Brookwater Circle
College Station, TX 77845-8735
879-695-6616

The Magee-Johnson Family

The Steve Johnson family, from left to right: Jennifer, Nita, Steve, Bill and Ross.

Mississippi Baptist College Cafeteria

"Meeting Nita Magee, the Best Day of My Life"

"In preparation for my freshman year, I reported to camp (football) at Mississippi College three weeks before classes

118

began. I didn't know anyone on campus other than a classmate from Biloxi High School where I had played and two older players from Biloxi with whom I had played. "

"On my second or third day at MC, Lloyd Seymour, an upper class football player from Biloxi, and I had supper together after practice in the cafeteria. So, there we were, at our table, with our cafeteria trays with all the little bowls of various foods. We sat opposite one another eating, talking football, and all sorts of other nonsense. Suddenly, two pretty girls I had never seen sat down at our table. They had met Lloyd a day or two earlier. They were freshmen and new to the campus as well and came over to visit with their new friend, Lloyd."

"The girls had not yet gone through the cafeteria line, so they did not bring a food tray with them to our table. We struck up a conversation, talking about where we were from, why we were here, all excited about the beginning of a new chapter in our lives. Lloyd and I continued eating while we talked with the girls."

"As the conversation continued, I looked down at my tray to get a spoonful of my mashed potatoes. What I saw was a bit strange, IN MY BOWL OF MASHED POTATOES, I SAW A HAND. It was just sitting there. I didn't know what to make of this, so I said to the girl, 'Would you like a spoon?' As I held the spoon out to offer it to her, she looked at me, puzzled. I smiled and looked down at my bowl of potatoes with her hand resting in the potatoes. When she saw what she had done, she gasped, jumped up from the table, and ran out of the cafeteria slinging mashed potatoes off her right hand as she left. Her friend followed her out while Lloyd and I had the biggest laugh of our lives."

"A bowl of mashed potatoes was sacrificed, but I had just met the prettiest girl I had ever seen. This is how I met Nita Magee. I knew I had to get to know this girl better, so, after a few days, I asked her out on a date. We went to the movies. We've been on one long date ever since. That was 48 years ago, almost a half century, and I can say with all certainty that this is the best bowl of mashed potatoes I have ever had." Steve

Juanita Elaine Magee and Steven Winslow Johnson married August 11, 1972.

Trevecca Nazarene University Cafeteria

Pictured at Panama City Beach are (from left to right) in the back row: Bill and Kellye. In front are Chase, Cruze, Berkley and Mia.

The family is pictured after Bill's MBA graduation.

"I was having lunch with my girlfriends in the cafeteria at TNU one day and everyone at the table started talking about the new transfer athlete on campus and asked me if I had seen or met him yet...I replied, No! but quickly asked, 'What does he look like and what sport does he play?' Then as the girls proceeded to all describe this tall and good looking baseball player from Miami, I looked up casually from the table and there across the cafeteria, walking in front of the larger floor to ceiling windows, was Bill. I knew it had to be him! He was tall, oh! so handsome, and carrying a plate full of chocolate chip cookies. He had a certain swagger about him that clearly and quickly pointed out he was not from around here."

The Johnson family at the Miami Zoo. Pictured are (from left to right) in the front row, Mia, Jennifer, Nita and Chase. In the back row are Bill, Berkley, Cruze, Kellye and Steve.

I abruptly interrupted the girls as they continued to discuss him, and I claimed boldly, HE IS MINE!!! Of course, they all laughed, but as I watched him walk across the room that day, with his cookies in his hands, I knew we'd have some sort of connection. Soon after, a mutual friend introduced us. We chatted about class work, and he asked to borrow my notes. I thought! Well, that is a pick up like I've never heard before! We went to pick up the the class notes from my parents' house, and I will never forget! As we walked into their home, he immediately removed his ball hat and sat it on the table. I asked him why he did so. He explained to me that he did not want to disrespect my parents in their home. I knew at that moment he was a special guy…not only tall, handsome, and athletic, but a man of strong character. Might I add…one who loved chocolate chip cookies! We quickly fell in love—folks, I'm talking two weeks. And the rest is history! We have been married for almost 14 years now and share the most beautiful four children together.   Kellye

Kellye Danielle Staudt and William Derry (Bill) Johnson married July 23, 2005

Pictured in the back row, from left to right, are Bill and Kellye (holding Cruz). In the front are Chase, Berkley and Mia.

Education—A High Priority for Our Family

EDUCATION IS A NECESSITY for humans to understand who they are. They need to learn and know how to live in a civilized society. They need to know the history of their country and respect its constitution. They need to be prepared to live and work in a global environment

Derry and I graduated Mt. Hermon High School receiving our high school diplomas. We did not stop there because our future goals required that we continue our academic pursuits. Derry received his Doctor of Veterinary Medicine Degree in 1958 from Texas A & M College which is now Texas A&M University. Derry practiced Veterinary Medicine for 49 years along with teaching senior veterinary students at TAMU.

I received a Bachelor of Arts Degree from Southeastern Louisiana University on May 13, 1978; a Master of Education from SLU on December 20, 1980; and a Specialist in Education on May 18, 1984 from SLU. I served 27 years in education in Louisiana and Texas.

Juanita Magee Johnson and Steven W. Johnson

Our daughter, Juanita Elaine Magee Johnson, received a Bachelor of Science in Biology at Mississippi College in May, 1974; Associate of science in nursing at Miami Dade College; Bachelor of Science in Nursing at Miami Dade College, Master of Science in Nursing Administration and Leadership at Western Governors University.

Juanita received her Master's Degree in Nursing Administration.

Our Son-in-Law, Steven Winslow Johnson, received a Bachelor of Science, Business Administration in May, 1974 at Mississippi College; a Master of Business Administration/Finance in 1975 at Mississippi College.

Juanita and Steven Johnson's Family
Jennifer Jean Johnson received a Bachelor of Business Administration Degree at Florida International University on April 20, 2006.

Jennifer Jean Johnson

William Derry "Bill" Johnson received a Bachelor of Business Administration Degree in Accounting in May, 2005; and a Master of Business Administration Degree in Leadership in May, 2017 from Travecca Nazarene University.

Kellye Danielle Staudt Johnson (wife of Bill Johnson) received a Bachelor of Science, Sports Management with an emphasis in Marketing in May, 2004 at Union University.

Ross Melvin Johnson received a Bachelor in the Art of Accounting from Ave Maria University on May 5, 2016.

Ross in his Ave Maria football uniform.

Ross' high school graduation with Derry (left) and Dora (right).

Pictured at Ross' college graduation (left to right) are Bill, Jennifer, Steve, Nita and Ross.

Ross visited De Dee in College Station, TX.

Family wearing their university T-shirts. In the back row (left to right): Jennifer, Bill, Steve and Ross. Front row: Mia, Dora, Nita and Derry

Mt. Hermon High School Golden
Graduates

EARL S. WILKES AND WILLIE MARIE BURCH WILKES were graduates of MHHS. Their seven children also were graduates of MHHS: Bobbie Earl, Gwendora, Dorothy Elaine, Faye Ellen, Janice Marie, Kathy, and Earl S. Wilkes, Jr.

Each year on the first Saturday in May, all graduates of Mt. Hermon High School of 50 or more years, spouses or guest, and all teachers who taught at MHHS prior to 1969 are invited to attend the Annual Reunion of Golden Graduates held at the MHHS.

A scholarship fund was established by the Golden Graduates of Mt. High School. Each year a scholarship in the amount of $600 is awarded to a deserving graduating senior of Mt. Hermon High School. The recipient is selected by the principal and the Golden Grads Scholarship Fund Committee. The recipient must provide verification of maintaining a "B" average the first semester while attending a college or university. The Golden

Grads Scholarship Fund Committee must receive this verification no later than February 15 of the year. Members are encouraged to donate to the scholarship fund.

Wilkes children who attended the Golden Grads Annual Reunion on May 5, 2018 are shown in the picture below. Earl S. Wilkes "Chuck" and his wife Rebecca Wilkes will be the next Wilkes family members to qualify to join the Golden Grads.

Gwendora W. Magee, Faye Ellen Wilkes, Bobbie Earl Adams, Janice Marie Branch, and Dorothy Elaine Cook.

Two Life Pathways Meet

IT IS AT THIS POINT that I would like to introduce the Johnson family. It is compelling and intriguing to follow the similar paths of the two families as they intersect with the meeting of Steven and Juanita in their freshman year at Mississippi College in Clinton, MS. Let's begin with the life and legacy of A. E. "Bill" Johnson.

This story begins in a log cabin at the foot of Peppermint Ridge on Lick Log Lane which follows Buffalo Creek in the heart of the Great Smokey Mountains. It really begins decades earlier, but I'll pick it up here. This log cabin was the home of the Johnsons: Art "Pa" Johnson, Ruth "Ma" Johnson, and children, Gladys, Mattie, Verna, Dot, Joe, Ken, Harold, Bruce, Ross, and Bill – my Dad. That's 12 in all.

This log cabin, which still stands, with a roof of cedar shakes (as I remember from my visits) was approximately 10' by 15'. Out back of the house was a field which ran along Buffalo Creek where the family planted their crops which, through very hard work with few tools at their disposal, sustained their needs along with income derived from difficult and dangerous work in the nearby mills and factories when available.

A.E. "Bill" Johnson

Life was simple and hard. There was no running water in the cabin, no electricity, and no toilet. Drinking water was hauled in from a "spring" which appeared in the side of a mountain as the water made its way down from Peppermint Ridge into Buffalo Creek. Light was provided by oil lamps and heat by two "pot-bellied stoves" on opposite ends of the cabin. There was an "outhouse." "Refrigeration" was provided by a cave for dry goods, the cold, cold water of the creek provided refrigeration for things that needed to be kept really cold, and there was a smoke house for curing meat. I remember my Dad telling me how, when his Dad sent him out to hunt squirrels for dinner, he would be given a rifle and three 22 cartridges to bring in the dinner. He was expected to bring back three squirrels shot through the head so as not to spoil any of the meat. The family cemetery was about half way up the mountain on a little clearing.

My Dad, the youngest of the family, was born on July 6, 1927, which meant he grew up through the "Great Depression" on a dirt path (Lick Log Lane) in the Appalachian Mountains." There were many challenges, but no complaints. Everyone in the family, like in all families, contributed to the task of making sure that this family made it through.

The story, for my Dad, took a very sharp turn at age 12. His Father died of pneumonia and my Dad developed Rheumatic Fever. Now the family faced the remaining days of the Depression without its most important provider. My Dad was bedridden for a full year and he missed a full year of school. Afterward, he was very, very thin and had lost the ability to walk. He had to learn all over again.

This is where the American Spirit, fueled by opportunity and founded on the teachings of our Heavenly Father, is exemplified by the actions of this one, average and ordinary, proud, and poor mountain family.

The family recognized that this young man was not going to be able to meet the common, everyday challenges in the same way his parents and older siblings were able. So, they decided to pool their resources in order to provide a different kind of opportunity for their youngest than had been afforded them. Their education had been limited to grades 1 through 6 as this is as far as the local school went. This provided them with the education they would need to meet the needs of the work available to them. It was apparent this young man would need a different kind of education. He, likely, would not be able to stand up to the physical requirements of scratching out an existence in the Appalachian Mountains during a depression in his current state of health. So, with their efforts pooled together, it was off to boarding school for my Dad. As he progressed in school, he knew he had to "Do Good" with his family providing this extraordinary opportunity for him. As he grew older his physical strength returned to him. He graduated a year early as the Valedictorian and immediately volunteered for the Marine Corps as the country was still in the throes of WWII.

Following the end of the war, he was able to go to college with the help of the G. I. Bill. His oldest sister, Gladys, was married to a man, Leon Lewis, and they had just recently moved to Shreveport, LA. They offered him a place to sleep and a biscuit in the morning. He began his college education at Centenary College there in Shreveport. One year later, Uncle Leon's work took him to Oklahoma City. My Dad followed and continued his education here for one year. The next move was to Houston, TX. Here, my Father enrolled in the University of Houston, studying accounting. He lived in a garage storeroom converted into a one room "apartment" out behind Uncle Leon's house. While attending the University of Houston he worked as a night auditor for the United Gas Corporation. He graduated in 1950.

While working in the corporate headquarters in Houston, he would see a young lady reporting to work as he left work on his way to school. After graduating, acquiring full time employment with United Gas, and a respectable courtship, he and Betty Jean Henderson were married in 1950. I came along in 1952. My brothers, Don and Mike, came along in 1954 and 1958.

For my brothers and I, life has been dramatically different than it might have been had my Father's family not determined to provide a different opportunity for my Father. He moved up the corporate ladder with United Gas and eventually became the President and CEO of a small city gas company in Johnson City, TN. Under his leadership this company grew from a very small company serving a small city of 50,000 people to one serving customers in 13 states. He served as the president of the National

Association of Manufacturers, a behemoth organization of the country's greatest manufacturing businesses. His civic duties were to many to list, including serving as the chairman of many boards of directors involved in the building of a medical school and development boards in education, banking, and business.

Betty Johnson

I mention some of his accomplishments only because all of this, and more, was made possible by his own dedication and efforts, but also, the dedication and efforts of his family back in those hills in North Carolina. Their selfless efforts not only changed his life, but the lives of his children, grandchildren, future generations, and the countless people he served throughout his career.

I truly believe this is just one example of vast numbers of great opportunities this country offers if approached in the right manner. Learning to be productive and helping those with whom one comes in contact will change lives for coming generations. My children, my grandchildren, and generations to come along with many others outside of our family have benefited, and will benefit, from the generosity of these people they have never met.

Written by Steven Winslow Johnson, oldest son of A. E. "Bill" Johnson and Betty Jean Henderson Johnson.

My Life Continues.......

UPON DERRY'S DEATH ON JUNE 3, 2015, I became a widow. I have always felt God's special hand on me and especially during Derry's illness and death. God commands us to care for orphans and widows. When He gave the Law to Moses and the Israelites, He gave instructions on how to treat the orphans and widows among them—with harsh consequences promised if they failed in their responsibility. We find in Exodus 22:22-24: *"Do not take advantage of a widow or an orphan. If you do and they cry out to me, I will certainly hear their cry. My anger will be aroused, and I will kill you with the sword; your wives will become widows and your children fatherless."* In the New Testament, James says that taking care of the needs of orphans and widows is part of religion "pure and faultless" James 1:27. Caring for those in distress is not optional for followers of Christ.

I believe when God took my husband, God became my husband. When people ask me, "How are you doing?" I respond, "I am doing wonderfully well! God is my husband, and he is doing a great job of guiding and protecting me." I have heard it said, "If you choose to harm someone, don't harm a widow because you will be dealing directly with God."

After Derry and I had moved to College Station, TX, in 1990, Derry and I enjoyed traveling back to Kentwood where we had lived for 32 years. We kept our home in Kentwood for 28 years, returning every three or four months to keep it maintained. After we sold our Kentwood home in 2006, we stayed with family members in and around Franklinton which is 25 miles east of Kentwood. We always visited Franklinton the third week of October during the Washington Parish Fair which allowed us to visit with hundreds of family members and friends.

We did not want to continue inconveniencing our families during these visits; therefore, I had asked around two or three years trying to see if there was something that we could rent or purchase for us and for Nita and her family when they come in October or at other times.

When Derry was near the end of his life, he expressed a wish to remain in our home in College Station. I assured him that he would remain at home until God called him home. He stated, "After I am gone, you and Nita can do what you would like to do." Several months after his death, I knew that God was leading me to go back to Franklinton, my hometown and nine miles from I was born and raised and 25 miles from Kentwood where Nita grew up and where our grandchildren spent several summers there playing with cousins nearby.

Wisdom from many stated that a widow/widower should not make a move for a year and should be careful about moving where the children are because they could possibly move.

Returned to My Roots

GOD WAS DEFINITELY GUIDING ME in this search for a house in Franklinton, nine miles from my birthplace in Washington Parish, LA. In Texas, I had begun looking on the internet for houses for sale in the Franklinton area. I checked the realty listings every two or three days for weeks.

On this special day, when I clicked on the real estate listings, this Cottage listing popped out over all of the listings that I had seen before which seemed weird to me. I had called a realtor who is a brother to my nephew-in-law and stated to him that I was looking for a house to purchase on a small lot. I asked him to look at this Cottage listing and get back with me. He called to say that he could not show the property because the owner of the Cottage was the realtor and broker. I told him that I would be in Franklinton during the Christmas holidays and would be available to look at other properties.

I returned from Nashville on December 29, 2015, after spending Christmas in Nashville with the Johnson family. My sister Jan and son Al and wife Amy and I checked out some properties for sale that had multiple problems. My mind continued going back to the Cottage on Main Street. Janice knew the owners personally and set up a meeting for me to see the house.

I explained to them that I was planning to make a move to Franklinton to be near my four sisters and a brother and their families. On December 30, 2015, I rented the Cottage for six months and told them that I would purchase the Cottage after I sold my house in CS.

Two of my sisters, Bobbie and Janice, drove back to CS with me to begin packing. After three days, they had packed all of the items in the three upstairs bedrooms and pictures on the upstairs wall and were ready to return to Louisiana. After they left, I continued sorting and packing as I was preparing for moving into the Cottage. I drove to Franklinton on January 10 with D&D Moving bringing some furniture the next day. I slept in my Cottage that night and spent the remainder of my time unpacking until I returned to CS on January 23.

Upon my return to CS, I listed my house with a realtor on February 1. The house went on the market on February 3, and I spent from February 1 to March 14 preparing the house for sale. The house sold 90 days for cash after I had put it on the market. This was another example of how God was guiding my steps and taking care of me. I closed on my house in Franklinton on April 6, 2016. I was finally home after being away from Washington Parish for 64 years. I am living in my home at 1620 Main Street, Franklinton, LA, nine miles from where I was born.

"Thou shalt love thy neighbor as thyself"

In Matthew 22: 38-39—When one of the Pharisees asked Jesus, *"Master, which is the great commandment in the law? Jesus said unto him, Thou shalt love the Lord thy God with all thy heart, and with all thy soul, and with all thy mind. This is the first and great commandment. And the second is like unto it. Thou shalt love thy neighbor as thyself."*

God has blessed me with many kind neighbors. A most unusual thing for me to experience living in my house on Main Street in Franklinton is being surrounded by three neighbors whose first names are "Scott." They are Scott Schwaner, Scott Reedy, and Scott Schilling.

Captain Scott Schwaner is my next door neighbor who has been a "God send" for me. An article reads, "Scott purchased the charming Acadian cottage with a large back porch. It sits on three acres of land in Franklinton, LA, about 70 miles across Lake Ponchartrain from *M/Y Lady Gayle Marie*, but it is worth the trip. It's so different. In this area, you are surrounded by water all the time. But, paradise everywhere we look, actually. When you go to the country, you're surrounded by things you don't normally see, like horses and deer, and a cattle farm next door. It's just beautiful, lovely. It's absolutely lovely!" At one time, Scott's beautiful house was owned by Judge Delos Johnson, Sr. and his wife, Mrs. Pearl Johnson. Mrs. Johnson was referred to by many in Franklinton as "Miss Pearl" who was highly revered. I am so sorry that I never got to meet "Miss Pearl."

Scott is Captain of *M/Y Lady Gayle Marie*, the yacht named for Gayle Marie, wife of the late Tom Benson. The yacht was specifically designed for Gayle and Tom Benson several years ago. Upon Mr. Benson's recent death, Gayle became the owner of the Saints Football team and the Pelican Basketball team in New Orleans.

I actually got to know my neighbor Scott when we met occasionally in our yards from time to time. When he came home from a yacht excursion, I shared small fig cakes with him that I had baked for the Homebound members whom I visit. On one of his trips home, he invited me to join him and his close friends, who are also neighbors, in a delicious dinner prepared by him in his home.

Scott has been so gracious and kind to me in so many ways. He allowed my contractor to extend my underground water drainage pipes to drain directly into the large drain on his property. This kind gesture has eliminated any future water issues for me on my property.

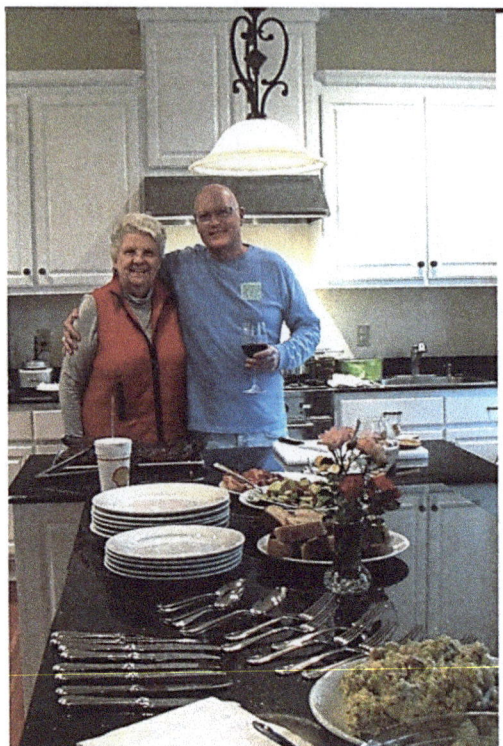

Dora and Scott Schwaner in his home for a dinner with neighbors.

Scott Reedy, his wife Rosemary and children live two doors down from me. They have been good neighbors, also. Scott R. continues to remind me to call him if there is anything that he and his family can do for me. Rosemary and I were raised on our family farms a mile or two apart near Silver Creek and the Bogue Chitto River. I have enjoyed trying some of the recipes in the Bowling Green Cookbook, 'Neer & Dear Country Fare that Rosemary gave me.

Scott Schilling and his family live in a large home behind me. Scott S. gave me permission to walk down his brick driveway for walking exercise to keep me from walking on the sidewalk with many fast cars and trucks traveling down Main Street.

Dora is holding a Saints football helment with Tom Benson's pictures honoring his memory.

Sherri Goss a next door neighbor invites me over to eat when they have a family gathering. Her sister Tracy will knock on my door with a serving of delicious fried yellow squash. One day I was setting up the ladder to climb to remove wreaths from the garage lights. I heard someone yelling, "Don't do that. I am coming!" She climbed the ladder and removed the wreaths for me. They really look out for me. What a blessing!

Dick and Marilyn Richardson are kind neighbors who live down the street from me. Dick, a cousin, learned that I was interested in genealogy and getting to connect with the people that I knew a long time ago. He made arrangements for me to go with him out to see Marjorie Jenkins (age 97) and daughter Margie Ann who own and operate the Jenkins Nursery. I saw large trucks loaded with huge oak trees that will become part of some landscaping design in a nearby city.

Marjorie and her husband, Bryant Jenkins, operated a dairy. In 1958, Bryant was one of Derry's first clients when he opened his veterinary practice in Amite, LA. Marjorie stated that Bryant loved Dr. Magee. Derry loved Bryant and the Jenkins family. He took Nita and me to their home one day where I remember sitting under that beautiful oak tree with limbs touching the ground forming a wonderful patio area. Dick drove me over to the house to see the amazing oak tree that is still standing and shading the patio as it did 61 years ago. Margie Ann shared with me that she has continued to take her animals to the Kentwood Veterinary Clinic for veterinary services.

Marjorie gave me a Chinese dogwood tree from their Nursery that will be planted in the corner of my backyard. I mailed copies of pictures that I made that day at their nursery and a copy of our book, *A Veterinarian's Life and A Veterinarian's wife.*

I received a "thank you" from Margie Ann. It reads, "Dear Mrs. Dora, Thank you so much for the copy of your book. I have read it cover to cover and totally enjoyed it.!! Such a love story— I am so glad to have known you both." Always, Margie Ann "P.S. Come back for a visit soon. It was nice to see you."

Leah Johnson, a neighbor across the street from me, brought a quiche to my house soon after I had made my first move to my cottage in Franklinton, but I had already returned to Texas. My neighbor Sherri became the benefit of the quiche. Kay and John Williams, my neighbors, provided me with a bountiful supply of figs. Their request, "Please share these with Jan." My sister Janice Branch has been a friend of theirs for many years. The Williams really love and appreciate Jan.

Other special neighbors that I have are the Riverside Medical Center employees who provide medical services for me and many others throughout the area. A special blessing for me is having Dr. Robin Fabre, Derry's niece, serving as an excellent Internal Medicine doctor at Riverside Medical Center in Franklinton, LA two blocks from my house. She is my primary physician and really sees to all my medical issues. If I need help around my house such as climbing a ladder, she sends over her husband Shad Ellison who is always willing to help me.

I am blessed to have my sister Janice Branch and son Jeff as neighbors on the other end of Main Street in Franklinton. A friend stated, "Jan takes care of one end of Main Street and Dora takes care of the other end." I have three siblings, Bobbie, Elaine, and Faye who are my neighbors nine miles away in the Mt. Pisgah community. My brother Chuck Wilkes, and wife Rebecca check in on me from time to time. They live approximately 20 miles from Franklinton on a large farm near Kentwood, LA.

There are multiple family members: Burch cousins, nieces, and nephews nearby, friends in my church and in the town of Franklinton who are my "neighbors."

Chuck Wilkes and his wife, Rebecca, who is holding
their granddaughter, Gigi.

Gwendora Magee

MY CALL TO MINISTER TO HOMEBOUND MEMBERS

I HAD A DESIRE TO CONTINUE MINISTERING to the elderly people in the hospital and those homebound as Derry and I had done after our retirements in 2007. Upon my arrival in Franklinton, I told my pastor and other church leaders that I wanted to visit the Homebound. I began immediately visiting the Homebound and learned that they bless me more than I bless them. I share some homemade goodies such as fig cakes and chocolate chip cookies with them. We share our thoughts, concerns, and Bible verses that are meaningful to us. When they share a concern with me, I stop right then and pray with them about their concern.

On February 10, 2020, I drove to Dirt Cheap a few blocks from my house. As I was getting out of my SUV, my left foot began "surfing" on the small gravel covering the blacktop surface. I tried to stop by putting down my right foot, but I continued sliding. I grabbed the sides of the SUV and held on until my body reached the ground. I turned loose and just relaxed a minute trying to figure on how I would get up. A sweet lady who was passing by noticed that I was sitting on the ground and looked like I might need help. She asked me if she could help, and I quickly stated, "Yes." She came around to where I was located and asked a young man passing by to help. They stood me up and asked if I were o.k. I told them that I was fine and was not injured. I got into my SUV and drove away making two more stops before returning home.

I did not call Dr. Fabre nor did I go to the emergency room at the hospital because I was not injured. Approximately a week later, I began to notice that I was getting stiff in my left lumbar area and found sitting was very uncomfortable for me. I called Dr. Fabre, and she asked me why I did not call her when I fell. As I stated, I was not injured. She ordered an x-ray of my spine. She and the radiologist determined that I had arthritis under my left lumbar. On the x-ray, it appeared that there was white foam under the lumbar. Dr. Fabre ordered a pain prescription for me. I lay in the bed flat on my back which was a very comfortable position. But when I moved myself from the bed to stand, I experienced some pain in the hip area. When I walked and stood, I experienced. no pain nor discomfort. It was very difficult for me to sit, but I could stand as I prepared my breakfast, lunch, and supper. I was able to do my laundry and maintain the area where I was confined.

My sister Jan who lives a few blocks away came after school each day to check on me. She made trips to the pharmacy and grocery store to purchase things for me. She cranked my vehicle daily to keep the battery charged. I waited to shower until she was in the house in case I needed help. A friend Marye Dykes who helps me at times was very helpful. She helped prepare some meals for the freezer. She made trips to the grocery and pharmacy for me when needed. I finally reached a point where I could sit in a chair comfortably.

After the CORONAVIRUS Pandemic hit our nation and the world, our lives changed tremendously. Staying home and keeping social distancing was nothing new for me because I had been doing these things since February 15. I practice the guidelines set up by our National Task Force which includes washing my hands and wearing a mask when I go out in public places. Due to being 84 years old, I am considered to be in the most vulnerable population to get the virus. Even though I do not have any health issues, I remain diligent in trying to keep myself free of the Covid-19.

On Tuesday, May 19, I was able to see a Nurse Practitioner at Ochsner Hospital who gave me a thorough examination which revealed that I had no pain and no need for any other treatment. She discharged me and commended me on my excellent health. I told her that I had siblings who are amazing as they do things to remain healthy. Her comment, "You and your siblings have good genes." I quickly agreed and felt very blessed that our parents passed onto us some ways to remain healthy: work hard which gives us plenty of exercise, keep a strong faith in God, cook and eat nutritious meals, and demonstrate resillency. Our family motto is, "When the going gets tough, the tough gets going."

I look forward to continue serving the elderly and Homebound when the time arrives. I talk to some of them on the telephone checking to see how they are doing. Our churches, neighbors and Christians throughout our community are constantly checking on us to make certain that we have the things that we need. Our community is one of the millions of communities who are demonstrating the true American spirit in caring for its citizens. I thank God who directed my path to this town and community in the continuation of my journey.

MY NEW NEIGHBORS

JOHN AND ROSEANNE GANLEY and their daughters, Maddie and Ellie, who moved from the Woodlands, TX became my new neighbors in July, 2019. Maddie is attending Tulane University and Ellie is at Bowling Green School. They purchased the Johnson house next door sometimes referred to as "Miss Pearl's house" from Captain Scott Schwaner.

The Ganley family is very caring and sensitive to the needs of others. John took on the responsibility of rolling my garbage can to the street on Wednesday afternoons and returning it on Thursday after the garbage truck emptied the cans.

On two occasions when I was hosing down my front porch, I became locked out of my house due to the latch not working properly. In my wet clothes and in my barefeet, I walked over to the Ganley's house to use their telephone to call my sister Jan who has a spare key to my house. They were so cordial and kind offering me cold water and calling my sister. After these episodes of being locked out of my house, I have had a new door lock installed and a spare house key placed where I can get myself in the house without inconveniencing the neighbors and my sister Jan.

Occasionally, Roseanne comes by for a visit after work or on one of her days off. We enjoy talking and getting to know each other. I was born and raised nine miles from Franklinton and attended Mt. Hermon High School where Roseanne's mother attended and was a classmate of my sister Elaine Cook. Roseanne grew up in Franklinton and graduated Bowling Green School, about two blocks for our homes. I am 30 years older than Roseanne which is the reason our paths did not meet in Washington Parish until now.

In another part of this book, I tell the story of how Roseanne was instrumental in getting the cancer in my mouth diagnosed. I am very blessed to have them as my next door neighbors.
HURRICANE IDA brought neighbors together!

My neighbors, Lucy and Brannon Breland, live across the street from me. They demonstrated the true "neighborly spirit" after Hurricane Ida left limbs and debris in our yards. After completing the clean-up in their yard, they came over and helped my daughter Nita and me clean-up my yard. Lucy joined us in picking up limbs, and Brannon came over with his leaf blower which helped to expedite the clean-up.

My Journey took another unexpected

turn...

DUE TO THE DIFFICULTY of inserting my bottom denture, I realized that something was wrong in my left jaw. I called Dr. Roseanne Ganley, my neighbor, who is a dentist in Franklinton. She saw me on Wednesday, January 20, 2021 at 4:00 p.m. and realized that I had a problem. She immediately called Dr. Ben Almerico, a dental surgeon in Covington, LA, and scheduled an appointment for me on January 29 at 11:45 a.m. After examining my mouth, he diagnosed the problem as Squamous Cell Carcinoma. Cancer was something I had always feared and dreaded.

One of the reasons for my anxiety was the distance to the doctors and hospitals in Covington, 25 miles from Franklinton. I knew there would be many required trips to Covington. My daughter and son-in-law and two adult grandchildren live in Miami, FL. My other grandson and his family live in Nashville, TN.

Several years ago, I was diagnosed with Macular Degeneration. I have the ribbon effect in my left eye which hinders my ability to read and write. I knew that I could not drive safely in a city where traffic is moving in all directions. I am able to drive in my town and surrounding community. The Ophthalmologist told me that I would never lose my sight which was a great comfort to me.

In visiting with Dr. Ganley, I had expressed concern about not having family nearby to take me to doctor appointments. Nita is so faithful to be with me when I need her, but I knew that she could not always be available for transporting me to Covington.

Roseanne realized my concern about transportation and stated that my transportation would be provided by her, and if she is working on the day of a doctor appointment, her husband John would transport me.

Roseanne drove me to my appointment with Dr. Almerico. While we were in his office, he called Dr. Kevin McLaughlin, M.D., D.A.B.S.M. board certified Otolaryngology and Sleep

Medicine. Dr. McLaughlin agreed to see me that afternoon after office hours. Roseanne and I decided to wait as long as necessary to expedite the process of getting a biopsy to the lab to determine the next step.

Dr. McLaughlin saw us around 5:00 p.m. on January 29 and began a thorough examination of my mouth and left jaw. He took a biopsy that would be sent to the lab on Monday. Lab pickup had already been done that day. He stated that as soon as he received the results, he would schedule a PET Scan which would determine the approach to be used in my treatment. The PET Scan will determine the area of the cancer and let the doctor know if it can be removed surgically or if another treatment would be used.

On February 8, Dr. Roseanne Ganley drove me to meet with Dr. R. Scott Bermudez, M.D., Radiation Oncologist at Mary Bird Perkins Cancer Clinic to begin planning for my Radiation therapy. He had requested that I bring someone with me. Being a dentist, Roseanne understood what was being communicated and took very good notes. On the referral from Dr. McLaughin on January 29, Dr. Bermudez, Radiation Oncologist, began making plans for my 30 radiation treatments. I was blessed to have my niece Rebekka Stafford available to transport me to appointments. She could and was willing to do anything for me. She has much medical knowledge and knows the ins and outs of hospitals, spending months in a Baton Rouge Hospital with her daughter Hannah who was seriously injured in a car wreck. Rebekka made trips to the pharmacy and grocery stores for me. She lives near me and made visits to my house checking on me periodically.

On February 11, Rebekka accompanied me to Mary Bird Perkins for the PT/CT Scan. As soon as we had the scans, we took the disks to Dr. McLaughlin's office as we had promised. Rebekka and I met with Dr. McLaughlin to learn about my options for treatment. After hearing these options, I know the Holy Spirit was guiding me as I immediately expressed a desire to have the cancer removed surgically as soon as possible. Dr. McLaughlin stated that he did not have any openings during the next two weeks, but he could perform surgery the following day which was on Saturday, February 13.

We agreed, and I looked at Rebekka and asked if she could bring me on Saturday. She said that she could. The doctor told us to be at St. Tammany Hospital at 5:00 a.m., and we were.

After the surgery was set, Dr. McLaughlin began making arrangements with the Hospital staff to prepare for the Saturday surgery. They asked to see my Covid Vaccination Card. At age 85, I have no medical issues which would have required prescription medications. Had I been on medications, the medical staff could have had a reason not to do surgery on Saturday. But, that did not happen. Praise God!

Rebekka immediately notified my daughter, Juanita Johnson, R.N., of the surgery that was scheduled the following day on February 13. Nita began making flight arrangements from Miami, FL to arrive in Louisiana as soon as possible. Rebekka kept Nita informed of the progress during the six-hour surgery.

The tumor was a poorly differentiated Squamous Cell Carcinoma. The diagnosis was Malignant neoplasm of the left cheek mucosa in the left Buccal (cheek). Cancer was removed in lymph nodes.

I understood the cancer is fast growing but was not attached to any outlying body tissues. Due to one side of the tumor extending a little farther than the other sides, it was determined by the doctors to prescribe radiation treatments. These radiation treatments would make certain any cancer cells lurking in the area would be eradicated.

I was discharged on Sunday morning, February 14, and arrived at my home in Franklinton at noon. My sister Janice Branch and niece Pam Forrest met Nita at the Baton Rouge airport, transporting her to my home in Franklinton. They arrived at my house at approximately the same time Rebekka and I arrived from the St. Tammany Parish Hospital.

Rebekka had notified First Baptist Church Franklinton pastors, Dr. Cody Warren and Bro. Joey Miller. They reported that they would be personally praying for me and again on Monday at their staff meeting. I received numerous phone calls from these pastors praying with me. Due to the Covid Virus, home visits were not encouraged, but Dr. Cody did make a home visit to pray with me. I received many cards from Christian family and friends, and Sunday School classes. I was very much covered in prayer by so many who were praying for my healing.

Their prayers voiced over the telephone were very personal and meaningful. Grandson Bill's family in Nashville shared that they were praying for me daily. Grandson Ross called to wish me well. Granddaughter Jennifer sent get well wishes through cards, e-mails, and telephone calls. Nita and Steve were prayer warriors for me during this time.

When Nita, an RN, arrived at my house, she immediately began applying her nursing knowledge and skills taking care of me. She spent several days with me monitoring the surgical drainage and treating the donor leg where the skin was removed for the graft needed inside my cheek. She made chicken broth to be used in preparing liquid meals that would keep me nourished. Nita drove me to my appointment with Dr. McLaughlin on February 19 where he removed the tube after Nita's report of the drainage meeting the specified requirements.

After spending several days taking care of me, Jan and Tam drove Nita back to Baton Rouge for her flight home in Miami, FL.

Nita refused to leave me until we had arranged for Marye Dykes to stay with me at night. Marye had helped me do many projects and was very familiar with me and my home. She agreed to spend the nights with me. After the first two nights, Marye told me that I was doing so well taking care of myself that I did not need her anymore. Rebekka kept Nita informed of my progress through pictures, texts or telephone calls.

Before I was discharged from the hospital, Nita requested Home Health whose staff would visit me, keep a record of my vital signs, physical therapy results, manage my prescriptions and keep Dr. Fabre, my primary doctor, abreast of my medical condition following the surgery. My great niece, Hannah Wascom was the Home Health nurse who visited me weekly and reported my progress to Dr. Fabre.

I engaged my great-niece, Haylee Brooks, a nurse at Riverside Medical Center, to come by twice daily during April and May to treat and dress the wound on the donor leg. Periodically, Haylee made pictures of the wound and sent them to Nita, Dr. Fabre, and Dr. McLaughlin.

Radiation Therapy Scheduled

THE RADIATION THERAPIST REQUESTED that I come on April 1 to make certain the Radiation "hat" fits. Niece Tam Brooks drove me to the appointment. I was informed that they would begin the radiation treatments on Monday, April 5. My first cousin, Linda Crain, drove me on Monday. My niece Pam Forrest drove me on Tuesday for the radiation treatment and to the facility nearby where they conducted the swallowing test before the radiation treatment got too far along.

At this point, I already had drivers lined up for the next two weeks. It did not take long for volunteers to sign up to drive me for the required 30 days of radiation treatments. During the last week of radiation treatments, only family members transported me. Niece Rebekka Stafford had a big part in arranging transportation to radiation treatments. My brother's wife Rebecca Wilkes drove me to a radiation treatment and a doctor visit. She did some grocery shopping for me.

As a Christian, I should have never feared or doubted that I would not have transportation to and from doctor visits and to the Mary Bird Perkins Cancer Treatment Center. I knew that God had promised me that he would take care of my needs, and he has been faithful to do that. I felt God's healing power and presence throughout this cancer journey.

Steve Johnson, my son-in-law wrote, "I trust all is well with you. We are so pleased to know that you are in the company of such well qualified and capable hands. It's comforting to know that you have so many people there who are willing and able to assist you in getting to and from your appointments and procedures. We are all praying for you and your healing."

Grandaughter-in-law Kellye Johnson, wrote, "Once again I'm so thankful you are surrounded by such amazing family and friends."

I received 30 radiation treatments during the months of April and May. As the radiation began doing what it was supposed to do in eradicating the cancer, I began experiencing some effects in my neck area. Provided by Dr. Bermudez, I applied Aquafor cream and "Sweet Cream" on the neck area that was breaking out in a burning rash. Because Marye Dykes had experienced several cancer operations, removal of lymph nodes, and several radiation and chemo treatments, I chose her to come twice a day for two or three weeks to bathe the neck area with hydrogen peroxide and apply the creams.

I awoke around 3:00 a.m. each morning with my pajama top stuck to my neck, requiring me to get out of bed and bathe my neck area with warm water and hydrogen peroxide followed by the application of the creams. Marye came around 9:00 a.m. and returned around 5:00 p.m. to repeat the treatments. After two weeks with Marye's help, I began treating the neck in the shower after my donor leg healed.

Following the cancer surgery, I continued my homemade liquid meals that Nita had been preparing for me. I supplement these liquid meals with the Protein drinks which contain a variety of vitamins, minerals, and protein. Because I could not wear my dentures, I have remained on liquid meals since my surgery on February 13. I could not even eat soft foods nor drink citrus fruit juices due to the burning of radiation in my mouth, tongue and gums. In fact, Dr. Bermudez stated that of all of his patients, I was the one who maintained constant weight during these treatments.

After the 30 radiation treatments had been completed, I was scheduled for a PET Scan to confirm that I was CANCER FREE. My nephew-in-law, Shad Ellison, Dr. Robin Fabre's husband, drove me for the scan on August 24. When we arrived, the therapist met me in the waiting room and asked what I had eaten for breakfast. As I began to name the breakfast items, she stated that I was to fast—nothing after midnight. The staff called the day before to remind me of my appointment but did not remind me to fast.

The nurses were able to reschedule me the following day for the scan. I asked Shad if he could drive me the next day, and he said he could. I really felt terrible about the inconvenience I had caused everyone involved. My suggestion to the staff: when you call to remind me of my appointment, please remind me to fast.

When I met with Dr. Bermudez on September 26, he was excited to tell me that I was "CANCER FREE." Praise God, I am cancer free!

Periodically, Dr. Roseanne Ganley checked to see if my mouth had healed enough to begin making adjustments on my dentures. On Wednesday, October 6, Dr. Roseanne made one of the final adjustments on my dentures. I can now eat most table foods, but I continue drinking Protein drinks to make certain that I am getting the proper nutrition. My taste has not fully recovered.

I felt God's presence with me as I traveled through this cancer journey. Psalm 23 is a special prayer of King David which I have memorized. Psalm 23:4 is a Bible verse that became very real to me during this journey. It reads:"Yea, though I walk through the valley of the shadow of death, I will fear no evil for Thou art with me: thy rod and thy staff they comfort me."

I know God was leading me to make such a quick decision when Dr. McLaughlin gave me three options for treating the cancer. My response was. "I want surgery, and I want it now!" I will always be grateful to Dr. McLaughlin and his medical team for being willing to do the surgery on a Saturday.
PRAISE GOD! I AM CANCER FREE!

My Journey Continues...

I HAVE CONTINUED TO REMAIN ISOLATED due to the Covid Virus. I have followed all of the precautions handed down by the medical community. I have been faithful to heed the advice of my doctors who are committed to keeping me safe during this time of healing from the cancer surgery and treatments.

Even though, I have been isolated from the public, my family, and my church family for nearly a year, I have remained faithful to study the scriptures, listen to Bible teachers and preachers, and listen to the CD's of the KJV recordings.

My heart still remains with the Homebound members of our church. I had to stop my ministry with them due to the restrictions placed on visitors to hospitals, nursing homes, and private homes. I have been able to visit with one member on the telephone who is able to communicate. In fact, this member wrote in her own handwriting the recipe of her Fresh Apple Cake a few years ago when she was approaching 90 years of age.

As I began to regain my strength, I baked this apple cake and took slices to her house. She was sitting on her front porch. She was so happy to see me, but I explained to her that I could not come in. I was bringing her some of the apple cake made by her recipe. Her son was in the yard and had assumed that I had come to visit her. He invited me in, but I explained to him that I could not due to my cancer surgery and treatments. I called her the next day, and she stated that she had one more slice left for her dessert at supper. She commented that this cake was much better than what she had baked in the past, but she was being gracious as she always is. Visiting the Homebound Members always blessed me more than I blessed them.

As I reflect on this past year and how God has healed me of the cancer, I have asked Him to show me what He has planned for me. I know He has a special plan for me, and I am willing to do whatever He asks.

I have agreed to continue serving as Director of our church's Homebound Ministry.

Recipes

Martha Washington Candy
(Dora's favorite candy to make)

2 lbs. confectioner's sugar (sifted)
1 stick butter
1 can condensed milk
1 -2 T vanilla
2 cups or more chopped pecans
½ bar of paraffin
1 box or 1 ½ packages of semi-sweet chocolate chips

Melt butter—mix with sifted sugar and condensed milk.
Add chopped pecans and vanilla. Roll or shape in small balls
(size of pecan halves)and slightly chill. Melt chips and wax in
double boiler. Dip candy pieces in melted wax and chocolate chip
mixture.
Top with pecan half before chocolate cools.

Wilkes Pecan Pie
1 cup light Karo	3 eggs
2/3 cup sugar	dash salt
1/3 cup butter	1 cup pecans

Bake at 325 degrees for approximately 50 minutes

Willie Wilkes Egg Custard Pie
9 " unbaked pie crust
3 eggs (slightly beaten with a whisk)
2 ½ cups milk—scald milk—being careful not to scorch
½ half cup of evaporated milk may be substituted for the ½ cup milk.
¾ cup sugar
¼ teaspoon salt
1 teaspoon vanilla
1 teaspoon nutmeg sprinkled on top
Bake pie at 400 degrees for 30-35 minutes. Test with toothpick for doneness.

Aunt Dora's Cream Cheese Pound Cake
1 pound butter   3 cups flour
1- 8 oz. cream cheese   2 T vanilla
3 cups sugar   dash salt
6 eggs
Cream together: butter, cream cheese, and sugar.
Add eggs-one at a time, beating well after each addition
Sift flour twice before measuring.
Gradually add flour, vanilla, and salt.
Batter will be thick.
Spoon out into well-greased 10" bundt/tube pan.
Bake at 325degrees for1 hour-1 hour 15 min.
Cake will not get real brown on top. Let cake
cool in pan for 10 minutes. Turn out on plate.

Jennifer Johnson's Pancakes
1 cup self-rising flour   1/3 sugar
2 eggs   1 T vanilla
½ cup milk
Mix well. Cook on griddle on medium heat.

Dora's Lemon Meringue Icebox Pie

Filling:

1 can sweetened condensed milk
½ cup lemon juice
3 egg yolks
Add lemon juice to condensed milk (little at a time)
Stir. Add egg yolks and mix well.

Meringue:

3 egg whites
6 T sugar (can use more sugar)
1/8 tsp. cream of tartar
Beat egg whites; add cream of tartar. Beat until stiff.
Add sugar and beat. Pour into a graham cracker crust.
Add meringue and bake in 350 degrees F. oven until golden
brown. Chill and serve.

Elaine Cook's Pralines

2 cups white sugar	1 teaspoon vanilla
¼ teaspoon baking soda	2 tablespoons Oleo
½ cup milk or Pet milk	2 cups chopped pecans
½ cup white Karo	

In a three quart heavy pot, mix sugar, soda, milk, and Karo. Use a
candy thermometer. Don't let it touch bottom of pot. Cook on
medium heat stirring constantly with a long handle spoon until
a soft ball stage. Add vanilla, Oleo and pecans. Beat until creamy
when it begins to lose its sheen. Drop on wax paper using two
teaspoons.

These pralines received the "Best of Show" at the 2015
Washington Parish Fair in Franklinton, LA. "Practice makes
perfect."

Willie Wilkes' Fig Cake

1 cup oil	3 cups all purpose flour
1 ½ cup sugar	1 teaspoon cinnamon
3 eggs	1 teaspoon nutmeg
1 cup buttermilk	1 teaspoon ground cloves
2 cups mashed fig preserves	1 teaspoon soda
1 cup chopped pecans	1-2 tablespoon s vanilla

Mix the above dry ingredients together in large mixing bowl.
Add oil to dry ingredients and beat well. Add eggs one at a time,
beating well after each addition. Add vanilla. Alternately, add
buttermilk and preserves. Pour into well buttered bundt pan; bake
at 350 degrees for 1 hour or until brown. Remove from oven and
let cool for 10 minutes. Then empty cake onto plate.

Granny Magee's Chocolate Pie
3 egg yolks
1 ¼ Cup sugar
2 T cocoa
1 ½ T flour or cornstarch
1 ½ Cup scalded milk

Beat egg yolks, adding a small amount of milk.
Mix sugar, flour, cocoa and add to beaten egg yolks.
Add hot milk and cook. Stir while cooking until thick.
Add 2 T of butter and 1 teaspoon vanilla.
Cool and pour into baked pie shell.
Top with meringue and brown in oven.

Meringue
3 egg whites
6 T sugar
1/8 tsp. cream of tartar
Beat egg whites and cream of tartar until stiff.
Add sugar; beat. Pour over cool pie filling.

Juanita Johnson's Hot Apple Cider
2/3 cup sugar
2 quarts sweet apple cider
4 cinnamon sticks
4 whole All Spice
2 Apples – Stick cloves in apples
Simmer ten minutes (maybe longer)
Strain

Photos

Bill, Jennifer, Juanita, Ross, and Steven Johnson at Ross's graduation at Ave Maria University, Ave Maria, FL, 2016.

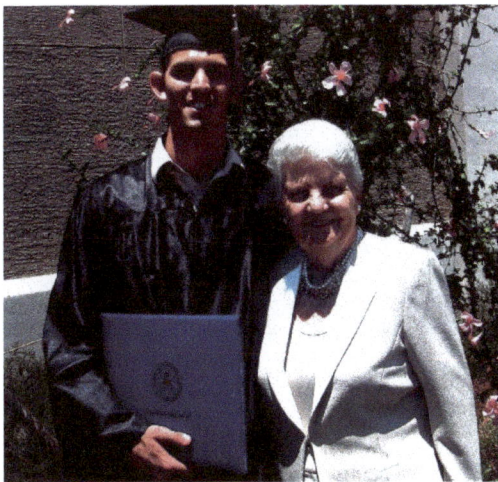

Ross Johnson and (Doe) Dora Magee.

Dora Magee, Juanita Johnson, and Derry Magee at Juanita's RN Degree graduation in Miami, FL.

Dora Magee, Juanita Johnson, and Derry Magee at Juanita's RN Degree graduation in Miami, FL.

Ross, Jennifer, Juanita and Steve Johnson at Jennifer's graduation, April 20, 2006 at FIU in Miami, FL.

Jennifer Johnson, Dora Magee, Bill Johnson, Derry Magee, and Ross Johnson attended Bill's graduation at Palmetto High School in 1999.

Derry Magee, Dora Magee, Bill Johnson, Juanita , Jennifer, and Ross Johnson at Bill Johnson's graduation at Travecca Nazarene University in May, 2005.

Ross, Bill, Steve and Juanita Johnson, and Dora Magee with Bill in May, 2017 receiving his MBA from Travecca Nazarene University in Nashville, TN.

Juanita with son Bill Johnson in May, 2017 receiving his MBA.

Dora, Bill, and Derry at Bill and Kellye's wedding in Nashville, TN.

Dora and Derry celebrated their 50th Wedding Anniversary at Juanwood, in Kentwood, LA.

Derry and Dora Magee with Sandra and Gerald Wynn, dear friends from Texas for the Magee's 50th Wedding Anniversary.

Dora and Derry in front of their Brookwater home in College Station, TX.

Rebecca and Chuck Wilkes, fishing in their boat at Venice, LA.

Rebecca and Ross driving the boat to the loading ramp.

Dr. Robin Fabre, Juanita Johnson, Derry and Dora Magee at the Washington Parish Fair.

Jennifer, Ross, and Bill Johnson together at the Beach.

Bill, Steve, and Ross spending time together in Miami, FL.

Dora's home in Franklinton, LA.

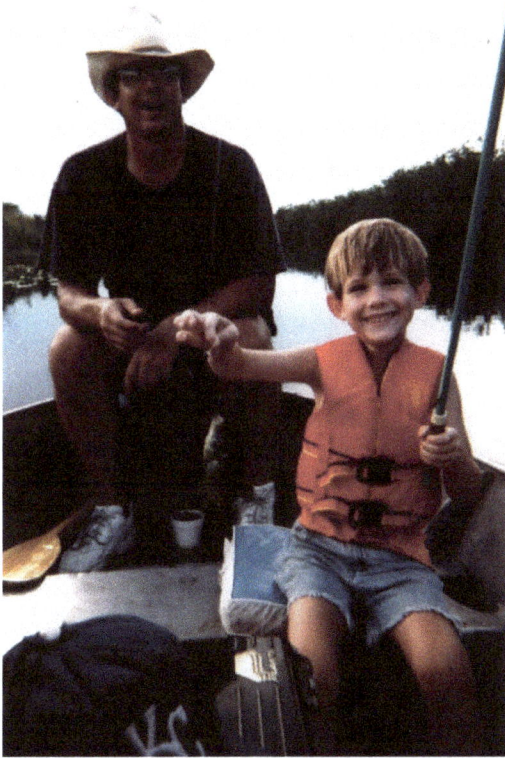

Ross is excited over his catch fishing with his Dad Steve Johnson in Florida Everglades.

Jennifer with her parents at her graduation at FIU.

Nita and Steve at Bill and Kellye's wedding in Nashville.

Jennifer with Ross at his graduation.

Dora and Derry's 50th Anniversary.

Dora and Ross at his graduation.

Kellye and William "Bill" Johnson wedding 7-23-05.

Dora Magee and Juanita Knight Alaska.

Dora and Derry Magee with his sister and her husband, Mary Jane and Nolan Fabre.

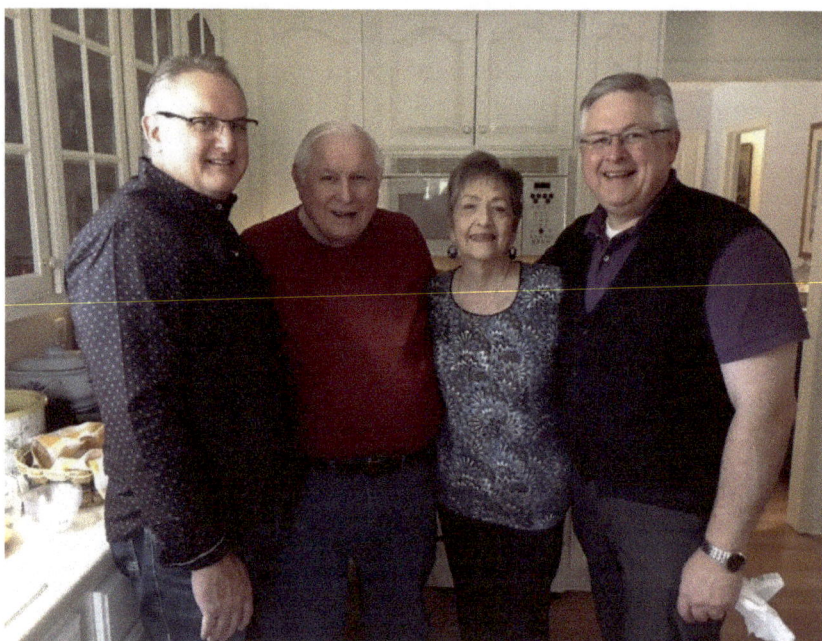

Andy, Velta, Bill, and Art Morris

www.ingramcontent.com/pod-product-compliance
Lightning Source LLC
Chambersburg PA
CBHW041718090426
42739CB00018B/3467